How to write what you want to say ... in the secondary years

a guide for secondary students who know what they want to say but can't find the words

Patricia Hipwell

First Edition published 2012

Second Edition published 2020

National Library of Australia Cataloguing-in-Publication entry

Author:	Hipwell, Patricia.
Title:	How to write what you want to say ... in the secondary years: a guide for those secondary students who know what they want to say but can't find the words / Patricia Hipwell ; edited by Charlotte Cottier AE and Katie Lawry AE.
ISBN:	9780987215925
Subjects:	English language--Rhetoric. English language--Semantics. Creative writing.
Other Authors/Contributors:	Black, Catherine Cottier, Charlotte Lawry, Katie.
Dewey Number:	808.042

Typeset in Delicious 11pt.

Text and cover design: Watson Ferguson & Company
Editing and proofreading: Charlotte Cottier AE and Katie Lawry AE
Assistance with the meanings of KEY TASK WORDS in Maths: Lyn Carter

Note: Text examples of the writing skill have been created to demonstrate that skill. Possible inaccuracies and out-of-date information in these texts are acknowledged by the author and do not detract from the validity of their inclusion.

Self published by logonliteracy

Printed in China by Everbest Printing Investment Limited.

contents

dedication

To my daughter, Elizabeth – the inspiration for this book. Since the publication of the first edition she seems to have had no trouble finding the words she wants to say.

introduction

This guide provides students with the language they need to write for a range of purposes. The book aims to provide students with a starting point to say what they want to say using language that mature writers use.

The book is set out in a double-page format:

- **The first page** includes a definition of, and things to know about, the writing skill. It also includes an **EXAMPLE** of the **SKILL** in a short piece of writing (with the sentence starters shown in bold).
- **The second page** provides the **SENTENCE STARTERS** and the language for **CONNECTING IDEAS WITHIN AND BETWEEN SENTENCES** to demonstrate the writing skill.

How to write what you want to say ... in the secondary years: a guide for those who know what they want to say but can't find the words (2nd edition) provides parents, teachers and students with a unique tool for improving writing. It suits students from the middle years of schooling to tertiary level.

key terms and ideas defined

task words (also known as cognitive verbs)	words used in questions to establish what is required in the answer and give a clear purpose for the type of writing required (see task word glossary on pages 67 to 72)
things to know	important information about the writing skill
writing skill	the purpose of writing; includes such purposes as describing, comparing, evaluating, justifying
graphic organiser	a template or visual plan that assists writers with organising their ideas and planning their writing
sentence starter	the opening clause of a sentence
connectives	words or phrases that link or connect ideas within sentences or ideas from one sentence to the next
formal language	language that is more characteristic of how we write than how we speak; does not contain colloquialisms or slang; adheres to the conventions of print – grammar, spelling and punctuation are correct
modality	expressing ideas such as possibility, certainty, frequency, and importance, using additional words to extend the main verb

analysing

meaning: the process of identifying and examining the parts of something in detail and discussing or interpreting the relationship of the parts to each other and to the whole; may involve description, comparison, explanation, interpretation and critical comment to determine the logic or reasonableness of the information

things to know: Analysing is one of the most difficult writing skills because it is not simply one skill. An analysis may begin with a description of what is being analysed. This is followed by identification of the parts and the relationship between the parts. This may involve comparing elements, looking at a relationship such as cause and effect where one thing leads to other things, evaluating the significance of parts or making inferences or interpretations. There is certainly no one clear way to analyse.

example – analysing whether polar bears could survive in Antarctica

There are a number of issues to think about when deciding whether a polar bear could survive in Antarctica. **Although** Antarctica is cold and icy like the Arctic, where polar bears come from, the two environments **are not exactly the same. One concern is** the temperature, as Antarctica is even colder in some areas than the Arctic. Polar bears **have** thick fur, **which would** provide them with excellent insulation and camouflage in Antarctica, **but** even this might not be enough to survive the freezing inland.

Another thing to consider is the polar bears' diet. There is no vegetation in Antarctica, **whereas** polar bears usually have access to berries or grass. **On the other hand**, Antarctica has plenty of other food for the bears, including seals, penguins and walruses. Polar bears are extremely strong. They are capable of throwing 250-kg seals out of the water, **so** they would easily be able to catch the seals and other animals in Antarctica. Polar bears would also have no other predators in Antarctica, whereas they usually have to compete with Arctic wolves for food. **While** this might seem like a good thing at first, the polar bears could quickly and easily hunt so many Antarctic animals that these seals and penguins become endangered. **This would mean that, in the end,** the polar bears would run out of food to eat.

Some other possible threats to polar bear survival in Antarctica **include** being hunted by humans and infection by local parasites. Although hunting the polar bear could be made illegal, it would not stop some people from killing the polar bears for sport. **Another problem is that** the polar bear is susceptible to the Trichinella parasitic roundworm, **which is** common in Antarctica.

Considering all these points, the polar bear may survive for a short time in Antarctica **but** would not be able to live there permanently.

sentence starters

..., and this interpretation has been achieved by ...
... could be broken down in the following way/s:
... effectively combines ... and ... with ...
... have ..., which would ..., but ...
... is a key component/distinctive feature of ...
... is also offered by ...
... is composed of/combines with ...
... is used to create ..., and this makes ...
... is (well) worth considering as a/an ... because ...
... leads to many ...
... perhaps representing ...
A ... can be broken up into three main parts, each of which ...
A further disadvantage/benefit is that/is related to the ...
All the elements combine to create a powerful message, which is ...
Although ..., ... are not exactly the same.
Analysis of the sources reveals that there were a number of causes of ...
Another benefit of this type of ... includes ...
Another problem is that ...
Another thing to consider is ...
Considering all these points, ... but ...
Even though ..., it does ...
It is, however, worth noting that ...
Of interest is that a ...
One concern is ...
Over time ...; this improves ...
Some other possible threats (to ...)/problems (with ...)/issues/causes for concern are/include ...
The main similarities/differences between ... and ... are ...
There are a number of issues to think about when deciding if ...
There are, therefore, ..., although ...
There is a complex relationship/strong connection between ... and ...
There is very little relationship between ... and ...
These and many other issues give us ...
This is because the ...
This would mean that, in the end, ...
Thus, the complex relationship between ... and ... develops the ...
While there are many benefits associated with ..., benefits to ... are not as significant as ...

connecting ideas within and between sentences

also; although; and; and this/that; as well as; because; but; by; combine; comprises; consequently; contributes to; consists of; create/s; depict/s; differ/different; draws the; enhance/s; even if/though; finally; for as long as; for example/instance; furthermore; hence; highlight/s however; if ... then ...; in addition; in other respects; in the same way; is made up of; is similar to/different from; not only ... but also ... ; on the other hand; provides; reflect/s; shows the/that; signal/s; so; some; specifically; symbolise/s; than; the reason for ...; therefore; this improves; thus; unless; when ... then ...; whereas; which is/allows/gives; while; yet

arguing

meaning: presenting one or both sides of an issue, idea or case to reach a conclusion; may involve the use of persuasive techniques (logical rather than emotive) to convince others that your opinion, point of view or argument about something is valid; also includes reasons to support an argument

things to know: Arguments are developed from issues of interest to particular groups of people or the population as a whole. The arguments and evidence to support those arguments are often drawn from research and academic texts. Personal opinions and subjective statements may be used but should be supported with solid evidence from a variety of sources.

example – arguing that ancient artefacts should be returned to their place of origin

During colonial times artefacts were taken from Australia, New Zealand, Canada and the United States to other places in the world. They were stored in private collections, museums and other places for scientific study. Some of these artefacts were very valuable. Other artefacts were important for what they told us about the past. Even some human remains, such as skeletons, were removed.

But these are no longer colonial times.

Thirty years ago, indigenous peoples from Australia, New Zealand and North America began to ask for these artefacts to be returned to their place of origin (repatriated). **Some people think that** these artefacts should be repatriated; **other people think that** they should stay where they are. **Here are some of the reasons why**.

The artefacts were taken without permission; **therefore**, they were stolen. **However**, UNESCO (United Nations Educational, Scientific and Cultural Organization) says that anything taken before 1970 was taken legally and does not need to be returned.

Repatriation is the right thing to do because artefacts belong in the place that produced them. The artefacts have a connection or link with the country of origin. They do not belong anywhere else. **On the other hand**, some people believe that they are going to be better looked after where they are.

If the artefacts are returned, **then** tourists can go and look at them. This will make money for the country of origin. **Alternatively**, the big museums of the world attract millions of visitors each year. **Therefore**, more people can appreciate the artefacts if they remain in museums.

The return of artefacts **is a controversial issue. People disagree on what should be done. This issue will be debated for many years to come.**

sentence starters

(State point of view). While several convincing arguments support this point of view, the balance of the argument is weighted in favour of ...
... also improves.
... as the issue is viewed from several perspectives.
... cannot always detect ...
... do not convey the ...
... has/have been vehemently opposed to ...
... has/have changed ... and not necessarily for the better/worse.
... is a controversial issue.
... is more likely to lead to ...
... is not just about ... If it were, then it could be argued that ...
..., it is important that ...
Evidence of this ... was shown when ...
Firstly, let us consider the argument that ...; this is easy to state but difficult to substantiate.
Here are some of the reasons why.
However, ignoring the detrimental effects that/of ... will be costly as the damage may be irreversible.
However, the issue of ... raises grave concerns about ...
In recent years opinion has become much more divided on the issue of ...
It is questionable whether there is any real need to ...
It is surely more important that ...
Making ... would increase/reduce the pressure on ...
Nothing polarises opinion in quite the same way as the issue of ...
People agree/disagree on what should be done.
Some people think that ...; other people think that ...
The decision to make ... is well supported by compelling evidence.
The evidence that supports the argument is accurate/credible/reliable/unreliable/ difficult to substantiate.
The issue of ... appears straightforward; however, closer inspection reveals compelling arguments both for and against ...
The issue of ... is controversial because ...
The issue will be debated for many years to come.
There are so many ... that it is difficult to know which ...
There is a great deal of evidence to/many studies that support ..., not least of which is ...
There is nothing that polarises opinion more than ...
This issue will be debated for many years to come.
We are much more likely to ..., and this has had an adverse/positive effect on the quality of ...
While this can be achieved without ..., being able to ... brings many advantages.
Without question, ... However, the issue of ... raises grave concerns.

connecting ideas within and between sentences

absolutely; admittedly; alternatively; at one level; because; beyond doubt; by contrast; conversely; despite this; even though evidence suggests; finally; furthermore; hence; however; if ... then ...; in addition; in conclusion; inevitable/inevitably; in spite of; moreover; nonetheless; obvious/obviously; of course; on the contrary; on the one/other hand; one reason for; so; such as; there are many reasons for; therefore; this/that; this is because; ultimately; whereas; while; without question

classifying

meaning: grouping things or people with shared qualities or characteristics into sets, or deciding to which set or category they belong, based on common criteria

things to know: Classifying objects or things can help to order and organise information. Classifications can be closed, that is, according to given criteria or attributes, or they can be open. This is where the classifier decides on the criteria for sorting or classifying the objects. Although it is also common to classify people, this can lead to labelling and stereotyping.

example – classifying the effects of bullying

The effects of bullying can be long-lasting and many victims claim that they have been affected by bullying throughout their lives. It can be extremely damaging to all aspects of a person's life. It is a difficult cycle to break because often the bullied become the bullies as they do not know how else to behave.

The effects of bullying **can be classified into** three **groups**. **These are** physical, behavioural and social effects. **Common to all the** effects **in the** physical group **is** some form of harm to the body, either externally or internally. Some evidence of bullying is obvious, such as bruises, scratches and cuts. Other signs are less obvious, such as trouble sleeping, suffering from headaches and stomach aches or generally feeling unwell. Victims may fake illness.

Effects **included in the** behavioural/psychological group **are characterised by** significant changes to a person's mental state. They may lose interest in school, work or social activities and be unwilling to participate in these. Self-esteem is low, and this is compounded by feelings of anxiety and helplessness. Sad, moody and depressed states of mind may result in suicidal tendencies.

The last group of bullying effects **are those that have** an impact on the victim socially. School is avoided and marks may decline from lack of attendance, interest or effort. Victims are fearful of being in unsupervised environments where there is no safety in numbers and may be reluctant to walk to school or catch a bus.

sentence starters

... and similar to other ... in this group ...
... are also ... classified as ...
... are also included in this group.
... are/can be classified as/into ...
... are/can be classified as/into ... (number) groups. These are ...
... but ... in the same group have similar ...
... can be included in the ... because ...
... classified as ... are in this group because they ...
... in the ... group have a number of characteristics in common.
... included in the ... are characterised by ...
... is also classified as a form of ...
An alternative classification is ...
Another way of classifying the ... is ...
Based on ..., the following items can be grouped together like this ...
By far the largest groups are ...
Common to all the ... in the ... is/are
Despite the superficial characteristic of ..., this item/product merits inclusion in the category of ...
For the most part, ... generally ...
For the most part, the items in this group have common characteristics that include ...
In this group, the following have several attributes in common and these include ...
Included in the group of ... classified as ...
Inclusion in this category is possible because ... has the characteristic of ...
The ... is/are organised by/into ...
The classification of ... into ... assists/helps us to ...
The following are alike according to the criteria of ...
The following classification has been developed for ...
The following has/have the attribute/attributes of ... in common:
The inclusion of ... can be defended by ...
The last group of ... includes those that have ...
There are ..., and yet they can be classified into ... groups or categories based on ...
There are (number) categories of ... and these are ...
There is a/are clear difference/s between ... and ...; therefore, it/they belong/s in different categories.
There is another way of classifying ...
These groups are ...
They are usually to be ...
They mostly occur ...
This heading/These headings provides/provide a suitable classification for ...
This is a very large group; therefore, subcategories are needed.

connecting ideas within and between sentences

also; and therefore; and these are; but; commonly; for the most part; in all/many/most cases/instances; in common; in general; in this case/instance; is based on; mainly; mostly; normally; such as; tend to be; there are examples; usually; without exception

comparing

meaning: examining two or more things or people and noting the ways in which they are similar AND different; examining the significance of the similarities and differences

things to know: Comparing involves examining the similarities and differences between two, or among more than two, things. A comparison is not a parallel description; that is, avoid writing about one thing and then writing about another. The best way to avoid a parallel description is to structure the text around the attributes/qualities/properties/features of the things being compared. As you do this, draw attention to the significance of the similarities and differences.

example – comparing natural pearls with cultured pearls

Pearls are unique among gemstones because they are the only gemstones to be made by a living creature (an oyster or mussel). They require no special cutting or polishing to highlight their beauty and have adorned humans and clothing since ancient times. Pearls **can be** natural or cultured, and **it is the** process of the formation of these pearls **that is a significant difference between them**. Both natural and cultured pearls are formed when the mollusc develops a sac around an irritant or organism that lodges inside the shell. The creature secretes calcium carbonate in the form of nacre (mother of pearl), which builds up around the irritant. **This is where the similarity ends because** natural pearls form when the irritant or organism is introduced naturally with no human involvement. **On the other hand,** cultured pearls form when the pearl farmers introduce the irritant that triggers the nacre formation process. Cultured pearls are available for sale after a couple of years **whereas** natural pearls take about ten years to form.

Just as natural pearls are found in water, **so too are** cultured pearls. **However**, natural pearls are found only in salt water **in contrast to** cultured pearls, which can be found in both fresh and salt water. Natural pearls are rare and difficult to find, **whereas** cultured pearls are easier to locate because they are cultivated on pearl farms, most of which are located in Japan, Australia and Indonesia.

Another significant similarity is that it is difficult to tell whether a pearl is cultured or natural just by looking at it. Natural pearls are gritty and have layers similar to onion rings. **In comparison**, cultured pearls are smooth with no layers. Their shape **is a more** regular spherical shape (only about 10% are perfect spheres) **compared with** the irregular, non-spherical shape of natural pearls.

While both types of pearls are expensive, natural pearls can cost as much as ten times **more than** cultured pearls, which makes cultured pearls **relatively** cheap.

sentence starters

... and ... are different because ... is ...; however, ... is ...
... and ... are similar because they both are/have ...
... and ... have more in common than ... and ..., especially ...
... can be ... and it is ... that is a significant difference between them.
... does the opposite.
... have many features in common, and this is one of the reasons that they are confused.
... if they are better ...
... is ... compared with the ...
... is a more ... compared with ...
... making it more/less difficult to ... than ...
A and B are similar in several ways, including ...
A comparison of ... reveals ...
A final/major difference is that ...
Another significant similarity is that it is ...
By contrast, ...
Closer inspection reveals that, although A and B appear very similar, subtle differences exist.
However, ... is less/more ... than ...
In many ways A and B are similar, yet these similarities are often forgotten as the differences are given prominence.
Initially, there were no differences between ... and ..., but as time progressed, significant differences emerged.
Just as ... is/are ..., so ... is/are ...
Just as ..., so too are/does ...
Obvious differences exist between A and B, particularly ...
Opinions differ about ...
Specific differences exist between A and B, notably ...
The elements of ... and ... will be compared.
The features of ... and ... are similar, whereas the features of ... and ... are different.
The main difference between ... and ...
The most striking similarity between A and B is ...
The similarities between ... and ... are more relevant than the differences.
The similarities between A and B are insignificant when compared with the differences.
This contrasts with ...
This differs from ...
This has to be ... and is a/an ..., with both ...
This is similar to ...
This is where the similarity ends because ...
To understand the problem, it is helpful to look at the similarities and differences between ...
While ..., ... does the opposite.

connecting ideas within and between sentences

additionally; alike/like/just like; also; alternative/alternatively; although; and; as well as; both/by/in both/all cases; but; by contrast; by/in comparison; compares/d with; differ also; differs from; even though; except; however; in all cases/instances; in common; in comparison; in contrast to; in many cases; in most cases; in other respects; in spite of; in the same way; just as ... so ...; more/less than; nevertheless; not only ... but also; on the contrary; on the one hand; on the other hand; rather; relatively; similar in that; similarly; similar to; whereas; while (both/each/all); yet

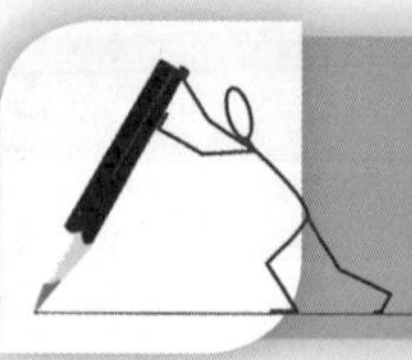

concluding

meaning: drawing together the main ideas of something and restating them in a succinct way, often as a decision; a conclusion may involve making recommendations for the future

things to know: Depending on the purpose for writing, a conclusion may be a summary of the key points made in the essay, contain a thought-provoking question or comment to leave the audience thinking, call for some action on the issue, contain consequences of a failure to act, or use a quotation. If you are restating a thesis and your arguments, practise saying the same thing using different words and phrases that retain the meaning.

example – drawing a conclusion about the role of the Australian Government in the national economy

There is general agreement that the Australian Government plays an important role in the national economy, **although** it is not as involved as the governments of many nations. **As well as** spending money on consumption and investing in savings, households and businesses pay money to the government in the form of taxes and rates and receive particular types of goods and services back from the government.

The government **is a key element in the** Australian market **for several reasons. Firstly,** the level of taxation taken by the government can affect the amount of money consumers have available to spend on goods and services. High levels of taxation can mean that consumers spend less and businesses cannot grow as quickly or employ as many people. Conversely, money collected in taxes can be spent on providing welfare payments. These payments, in the form of pensions and unemployment benefits, allow many people to purchase more as consumers, increasing income to businesses and creating jobs as businesses grow.

As well as the contribution that the government **makes to** provide welfare support, **it also** provides services such as schools and hospitals. These are paid for from taxes collected from both households and businesses. When the government spends money on infrastructure such as roads, schools and hospitals, it is providing money to businesses that do the actual building, helping those businesses to grow and employ more people. **In conclusion,** the Australian Government plays a significant part in the economy of the nation.

sentence starters

... and this is evident in ...
... are best summed up by ...
... but, all things considered, the advantages outweigh the disadvantages.
... investigated several ways that could ... and came to the conclusion that ... was the best option.
... is a key element in the ... for several reasons.
... provide a rare and firsthand account of ...
... reveal how ...
..., which were invaluable to those at the time because ...
A conclusion can be drawn from ..., this being ...
All the evidence is conclusive because ...
All things considered, the following conclusion can be drawn.
All this is known from the ...
An examination of all the data allows the following conclusions to be drawn:
An examination of the evidence allows the following summary to be made:
As ..., these ... have given unprecedented insight into ...
As well as the contribution that ... made/makes to ..., it also/led the way in ...
Audiences everywhere will enjoy the performance of ...
Clearly, it can be concluded that ... is the best and most cost-effective/practical, reliable, efficient ...
Consequently, it would seem better for/to ... than ...
Considering all the options, it would seem better to ... than ...
Even though ..., using a ... can be such a good place to start to ... that it is reasonable to conclude ...
In ..., it is clear how/that/why/when ...
It is appropriate/helpful now to make some concluding remarks/observations.
It would appear reasonable to conclude that ... and, therefore, recommend ...
On balance, the main conclusion is ...
The arguments discussed conclusively support the point of view that ...
The conclusion is by no means clear; however, ...
The latter/former was significant because ...
There is absolutely no doubt that this is the most valid/worthwhile conclusion.
There is general agreement that one significant advantage of ... is that it allows ...
There is general agreement that the ...
There is, therefore, some/no/considerable/much doubt that this is the best conclusion.
These are the final statements made here to support ...
Thus, in summary, ...
Thus, to conclude/in conclusion, ...
To sum up, then, ...
To support the conclusion ... arrived at, ... outlined the benefits of ...
When ..., then ... and, if ..., then ...

connecting ideas within and between sentences

accordingly; all things considered; although; as a final point; as well as; assuming that; because; clearly; conclusively; consequence/consequently; conversely; decisive/decisively; first/firstly; finally; if; in any case; in summary; inconclusive/ inconclusively; inevitable/inevitably; much doubt; no doubt; now; on balance; on condition that; overwhelming/overwhelmingly; second/secondly; so; some doubt; the final point; then; these/which include; thus; to conclude; we can conclude

contrasting

meaning: examining two or more items or situations and focusing on the differences, referring to both/all of the items/situations throughout

things to know: Unlike comparing, which means to examine similarities and differences, contrasting involves looking at only the differences between two or more things. Contrasting things systematically by examining the attributes of each of the things being contrasted gives a logical and thorough distinction between the two things.

example – contrasting concrete and Plazrok

Concrete is a traditional building material comprising aggregate (rock, sand and gravel), and a binder such as cement or asphalt and water. It is poured after all the ingredients have been mixed and hardens to form a very durable building material. **By contrast,** Plazrok is a modern, manufactured, lightweight aggregate made from the predominantly plastic material retrieved from landfill.

Both concrete and Plazrok are strong building materials. Concrete is widely used in houses, schools and other buildings because it is so cheap. Plazrok can be made into bricks and also be used as reinforcement for concrete instead of steel. **While** concrete is more brittle and prone to cracking, Plazrok does not tend to crack because it is more flexible.

Concrete is manufactured from natural and human-made materials. Rock, sand and gravel that form the aggregate in the mix are natural; the cement is a combination of natural materials and by-products from other manufacturing industries such as steel production; and the water, of course, is natural. Significant carbon emissions are associated with the production of the cement component of concrete. **On the other hand,** as Plazrok uses recycled plastic waste taken directly from landfill, fewer carbon emissions are associated with its production, **although** it could be argued that the carbon emissions associated with the production of the plastic in the first place are huge.

A notable difference between the two types of building material **is** transport costs. As a heavier material, concrete is more expensive to transport, leading to greater fuel consumption and increased carbon emissions. **Both** materials are durable and long-lasting. Plazrok is a particularly useful building material in areas prone to earthquakes, such as New Zealand, because it resists cracking. **However**, once concrete starts to crack and break up, it can be crushed and used as a cheap alternative to gravel.

* note the comparative adjectives – more, fewer, heavier, greater

sentence starters

... and ... are different because ... is/has ..., whereas ... is/has ...
... and ... are not alike in any way.
... and ... have far less in common than would first appear.
... and ... have nothing in common; only differences are apparent.
... are dissimilar from ... in that it/they has/have ..., whereas ...
... are much better at ..., although ...
... is an obvious difference between ... and ...
... is at variance with ...
... is dissimilar from ...
... is not like ... in any way.
A comparison of ... and ... reveals only differences.
A final difference is that ...
A notable difference between the two types of ... is ...
Another notable/noticeable difference is ...
Be careful not to overlook the hidden differences between ... and ...
By contrast, ...
Despite more similarities than differences, there are some specific differences that exist between ... and ...
Even though there are significant differences between ... and ..., with respect to ... they are strikingly similar.
Initially, there were no differences between ... and .... However, as time progressed, significant differences emerged.
Many of the elements of the two ... are significantly different.
Obvious differences exist between ... and ..., particularly ...
One/A major difference between ... and ... is ...
Opinions differ about ...
Slight differences appeared at first, and these became more noticeable over time.
Specific/subtle differences exist between ... and ...
The ... are different.
The distinguishing characteristics of ... make it very different from anything else.
The elements of ... and ... are different.
The main differences between ... and ... are ...
There are differences between ...
There is nothing about ... and ... that is in any way similar.
This differs from ...
While ... is like ..., ... is like ...
While ..., it is not as efficient/attractive/hardwearing/durable as ...

connecting ideas within and between sentences

admittedly; alternatively; although; both; but; by contrast; compared with; conversely; differs from; even so; even though; however; in any way; in contrast (with); in fact; in no similar way; in other respects; in spite of this; more/greater than; nevertheless; no commonality; not only ... but also; on the contrary; on the one hand; on the other hand; opposing; or; other differences; rather; unlike; whereas; while; with respect to; yet

describing

meaning: giving a detailed account (written or spoken) of the characteristics, features, properties, parts or qualities of something (event, pattern, process or situation) or someone

things to know: A description should be about the observed features. It does not interpret the meaning of those features (see the skill of interpreting on pages 36 to 37). A very detailed description should allow the reader to visualise what is being described. However, for most purposes, this level of detail is not required. Therefore, descriptions usually focus on the important features.

example – describing the characteristics of an effective public speaker

Glossophobia, or speech anxiety, **is the** fear of public speaking. The word derives from the Greek *glossa+* meaning tongue, and *phobos*, meaning fear or dread. Few people are born public speakers. Most people who have to speak to an audience have either been trained or done it so many times that it is no longer a frightening experience. **There are definitely techniques that** public speakers can learn and practise.

Some of the distinguishing characteristics of effective public speakers **are** that they are interesting, relaxed and comfortable. They focus on the 'speaking' part and not the 'public'; they deliver their speech as though it is a conversation between them and the audience.

Public speakers have the discipline to practise their speeches. They visualise themselves delivering a clear and interesting speech to their audience. They realise that the more they practise their speech, the more they will overcome their anxiety. **Another benefit of** practice **is that** it reduces the need to read out the speech. People who have rehearsed their speech are able to connect with their audiences to a greater extent than those who are unrehearsed.

It is unlikely that any speech will be perfect. Mistakes are unavoidable, and good speakers who make a mistake keep going because **even though** they realise that they have made a mistake, the audience generally does not notice. Making a mistake can work in speakers' favour **as it shows** the audience that they are human.

Another key attribute shared by many public speakers **is that** they include personal experiences in their speeches. Depending on the topic, they **may include** triumphs, tragedies, anecdotes and humorous interludes. Personal stories show the human side of speakers, and audience members can relate to these experiences because they may have had similar ones.

Finally, a good speech **is a** short speech! Always leave the audience wanting more. It is rare to listen to a speech and think, 'I could listen to that person all day!' It is more usual to be relieved when the speaker has finished.

sentence starters

... can occur as well as ...
... comprises the following characteristics:
... comprises/is composed of/consists of/is constructed of ...
... experience/s a number of ...
... has some/many distinctive features/characteristics that make it unique, including ...
... has some very distinctive traits, especially/including the fact that ...
... have many ... or distinctive features that have ...
... is made up of ...
... is similar in appearance to ...
... is unlike anything else seen/experienced previously, although ...
... looks/sounds/feels/tastes/smells like ...
... has a number of distinguishing/special/notable features, including ...
... has several distinguishing features, which include ...
(Also) of interest is that ...
An examination of ... reveals ...
An interesting feature of the ... is/are ...
Another benefit of ... is that ...
Another key attribute shared by ... is that ...
Important though ... is, it is not the most relevant factor in the description.
Most prominent/of great significance is/are ... that ...
Of great significance is ...
One/some of the distinguishing features/characteristics of ... is/are ...
Other important aspects include ...
Other less important/significant features are ...
The important/key/significant/major features/attributes of ... are ...
The major attribute of ... is ...
The most obvious feature of ... is ...
The most significant elements of ... include ...
There are definitely techniques that ...
There are several (noticeable) ...
This shows that ...
Typically, ... is/begins with ...
Upon examination, it is seen that ...

connecting ideas within and between sentences

additionally; all; along with; also; although; and; apart from; are a/the; as a result; as it shows; as shown in/by; as well as; besides; combines; even though; extra; extra features; finally; for example; for the most part; furthermore; however; in addition (to); (may) include; is a/the; is composed of; is made up of; It/He/She/They is/are ...; it is also; mainly; moreover; not only ... but also; rather than; several; show/s a/the; some; such as; the following characteristics; too; what's more

discussing

meaning: considering both or several sides of an issue or idea, without necessarily coming to a conclusion; supporting opinions or conclusions with evidence

things to know: Discussing is often associated with spoken language rather than with writing. However, in most of the writing done at school and university, discussing is a written debate where you are using your reasoning skills, backed up by evidence, to make a case for and against something – to consider the advantages and disadvantages of something. A discussion may include a conclusion but does not always, as it can leave the reader to make up their mind.

example – discussing the role of migration in modern Australia

When Europeans came to Australia in 1788, there were approximately 400,000 Indigenous people. The growth of today's population to over 25 million has been achieved, to a large extent, by migration. The history of migration is a rich one, from the first settlers who, as convicts, came here involuntarily, to the vast majority of migrants who seek a better life in this country.

Migration to Australia **increased dramatically during** the 20th century **and, since that time, the contribution of** migrant has been overwhelmingly positive. The world is on our doorstep; the Australian culture is rich and diverse; and cultural tolerance and understanding has improved. Migrants are generally willing to work hard to better themselves and are prepared to take lower paid, casual jobs. **This has the added advantage** of reducing labour shortages in certain occupations.

Many migrants prefer to live in the large Australian cities, **often because** it allows them to connect with their compatriots from their homeland. **This can lead to** overcrowding. **Other problems can result from** their unfamiliarity with the English language and the strangeness of the host country's custom and culture. **Consequently,** they may find that their own language and customs are not readily understood. **Of particular concern,** with the increasing emergence of crises caused by weather events or health threats **is that** some migrants may not readily understand the important warnings given.

Migration **provides** people who have skills that Australia may be short of, **and this contributes to** a healthy economy. Migrants often become very successful. The opportunities for language learning in the host country increase. With understanding and sensitivity, racial tolerance can be fostered, and relations between Australian and the migrants' home countries often improve.

One of the concerns about migration **is that** migrants may not settle, **especially if** they have been forced, rather than having chosen, to leave their home countries. **In addition,** many have limited English and may face employment challenges. Those who are employed are often unfairly criticised for taking over jobs. Those who are unemployed may require extra services.

However, despite some of the issues that occur as a result of migration, 21st-century Australian society would not be as rich and diverse as it is without the huge contribution migrants have made.

sentence starters

... provides ..., and this contributes to ...
A further issue for the future is that it is ..., making it ...
Another appealing feature is the ..., especially the opportunity to ...
Another disadvantage is that some ...
Another significant advantage is that it only ...
As with many other ..., ... can have ...
Clearly, the contribution of ... to ... has been overwhelmingly positive.
Critics of ... are concerned that there is ...
Despite some of the problems associated with ..., it is fast becoming an attractive alternative to ...
Further strengths of this ... are that it is ...; ...; and ...
However, as with many areas of ..., the future presents opportunities for/to ...
However, despite some of the issues that occur as a result of ..., ... would not be as ... as it is without ... the ...
In the past, ... has paved the way for ..., so may do so in the future.
It can be argued that ... advantages/disadvantages ...
It is a ... that comes with comparatively few weaknesses. The key ones are ... and ...
It is reasonable to assume/apply this finding to ...
Many believe that it is only a matter of time before ..., therefore, it is necessary to consider some of the issues associated with ...
Many of those involved in ... say that it is less/more ... than ..., especially ...
Of particular concern, ..., is that ...
One of the major concerns about/with ... is that ..., especially if ...
Other problems can result from ...
Proponents of ... argue that this ensures ... as there is ...
Several aspects of the issue need to be discussed, especially ...
The challenge will be to develop ... that can ...
The factors that contribute to this situation include ...
The move towards a ... should not be taken uncritically as there are several problems associated with it.
There are several possible explanations of this, including ...
There are significant advantages/disadvantages associated with ..., and many people have rejected ... because of these. They also mention how much ...
There is no doubt that there have been many advantages associated with ..., not least of which is ...
This can lead to ...
This does not mean that we should not be ... because it is possible for ...
This has the added advantage of ... in ...
This is compounded by its ...
While it seems inevitable that ... will rapidly/slowly become ..., we need to be mindful of all the issues associated with this.

connecting ideas within and between sentences

also; although; and; another; as a result; as likely as not; because; clearly; consequently; essentially; for example/instance; for the most part; furthermore; generally; however; in addition; in common; in general; in most/many cases; in the main; likely; mainly; many; more likely/often than not; most/mostly; most often; often; on average; on the one/other hand; on the whole; primarily; since; therefore; this; thus; to a large extent; typically; usually; which means that

elaborating

meaning: giving more information or detail about someone or something

things to know: Elaborating is not 'waffle' or repetition to increase word length. When elaborating, the writer should go into greater depth about the topic by including more details. The inclusion of definitions and relevant examples is a way to elaborate; so too is the inclusion of evidence (all supported by relevant quotes).

example – elaborating on the causes of homelessness

The word *homelessness* tends to conjure up images of people sleeping on park benches, under bridges, in back alleys and in shop doorways. **However,** homelessness can refer to rough sleepers who sleep outside and those living in overcrowded and inappropriate accommodation. People who couch surf – **that is**, sleep on couches in other people's homes – are also deemed to be homeless, and couch surfing **is often the first way that** some young people experience homelessness.

A number of factors can lead to a person being homeless. **Some of these work in isolation but many combine to make the problem of** homelessness **difficult to understand and even harder to solve.** Homeless people may be victims of drug and alcohol abuse or have a gambling addiction, which can plunge them into poverty. They have often been unemployed for long periods of time because they either cannot find work or find it difficult to hold down a job. When they cannot afford to pay rent, they are evicted and end up on the streets. **Even if** they can afford to pay rent, the general lack of affordable housing means there may be no houses or apartments available for them to rent. Homeless people often have poor physical and mental health. They may have been the victims of trauma and/or domestic violence. Sometimes people leave their homes due to a breakdown of family and other supportive relationships or because they feel unsafe living with others in the household.

The problem of homelessness **is a complex one, and** people who end up in this state are often without a support network of family and friends to help them through. There is a danger in seeing homeless people and thinking that it is their fault and they should do something about it, such as find a job and smarten themselves up. **If it were that simple, it is unlikely that there would be** as many homeless people as there are.

sentence starters

... are one example/are examples of ...
... is often the first way that ...
A cursory glance shows ...; however, closer inspection reveals ...
A detailed examination shows ...
A number of factors can lead to ...
Another benefit of ... is ...
Another key feature of the ... is the ...
At a glance ... is evident; however, a closer look reveals ...
At one level ... is clearly identified, but there is much more to discuss ...
Besides this/these ...
Careful observation reveals ...
Close scrutiny reveals ...
Finally, they are an efficient way of ...
For example, ... it/they provide/s ...
Generally, this/these ...
If it were that simple, it is unlikely that there would be ...
If the topic is placed under the microscope, then it becomes clear that ...
In addition to what is visible, other aspects are worthy of discussion.
It is referred to as a/the ...
It is/they are considered to be ...
Looking more closely, it is apparent that ...
One interpretation of the findings could be ...
Some argue that these detract from ...
Some of these work in isolation but many combine to make the problem of ... difficult to understand and even harder to solve.
The diagram provides additional information to the text, especially as it shows ...
The information is accurate and supported by the evidence, especially the fact that ...
The many advantages of ... include ...
The problem of ... is a complex one, and ...
There are a number of ways ... can be used.
There are ...; however, ...
There are more details to be examined and these include: ...
There is more to the topic/issue than it first appears; therefore, it should be looked at deeply.
They allow the ...
They are also useful for ...
They are made of ...
They can be adapted to ...
They demonstrate ...
This/These feature/s increase/s//decrease/s ...
Under these circumstances, ... would apply.

connecting ideas within and between sentences

additionally; albeit; also; and so; apparently; as revealed by; as well as; besides (these/this); clearly; closely; even if; examines; for example; for instance; for this reason; furthermore; generally; given this fact; however; if ... then ...; in addition; in detail; indicates; interprets; it becomes clear; it's clear; moreover; reveals; specially; specifically; such as; supports; that is; thus; under these circumstances

evaluating

meaning: giving a considered appraisal or judgement about the value or worth of something or someone by examining strengths, implications and limitations based on criteria and supporting this with evidence; making judgements about ideas, works, solutions or methods in relation to selected criteria

things to know: When evaluating, it is common to examine the advantages and disadvantages, pros and cons, positives and negatives, pluses and minuses or reasons for and against something. Evaluating usually precedes making a decision and justifying that decision. As well as an argument or proposal, a product or process can be evaluated using criteria, as can a historical source. In the Arts, evaluation is usually in reference to a given artistic purpose and is directly related to the analysis that precedes it.

evaluating an argument or proposal

example – evaluating the practice of taking a gap year

The decision to take a break (commonly known as a 'gap year') between school and tertiary study, or at some point during that study, is one that many students are taking. **The appeal of** taking a year or two (gap 'years' can be longer than a single year) away from study **lies in** the fact that it provides many opportunities, especially travel. The experience gained during the gap year can prepare students for university both academically and socially. **However**, unless the year is planned, it may be spent rather purposelessly. **Some have argued that** the gap year is the longest 'holiday' a person experiences in their lifetime*. **It follows that** serious thought should be given to the decision.

There are significant disadvantages with taking a gap year. Travel is expensive and a gap year can leave students short of money. **On the other hand,** there are many opportunities to earn money, and this can alleviate the financial pressures associated with university education. Taking a gap year **is worth considering as** an opportunity to gain new skills or to try some career options, including voluntary work. Students may take part of the year to prepare themselves for their courses by reading and gaining relevant work experience in their chosen field. **Nevertheless**, students will be 'out of sync' with school friends who have gone straight to university from school, **and this can be considered another disadvantage. Furthermore**, students may lose their university places, **especially** if they do not make their decision to defer clear to the university. Taking a gap year **is a viable option; however,** students should carefully evaluate the pros and cons **before** making a decision.

* Citation(s) providing the source(s) of this information or evidence for these assertion(s) would normally be included here.

sentence starters

... is a more suitable choice/option/solution because ...
... is a viable option; however, ...
... is more suitable/logical/ethical, etc. than ...
... is worth considering as/because ...
..., which is a significant advantage.
An examination of the options reveals that ...
Another consideration, often overlooked, is that associated with ...
Conversely, ... are more ...
Despite the criticism of ..., it is a viable alternative.
Economically/socially/environmentally/politically, the most outstanding benefit/disadvantage is ...
If ... is compared with ..., several differences emerge and these include ...
If ...; therefore, ...
Nevertheless, ..., and this can be considered to be another disadvantage.
Some would argue/have argued that ...
The appeal of ... lies in ...
The benefits are limited; the costs are significant, particularly those associated with ...
The following criteria will be used to evaluate the idea/proposal/scheme:
There are several flaws in the argument, and these include ...
There are significant advantages/disadvantages with ...
There are significant costs and benefits associated with ...
There are strengths on the one hand, and significant flaws on the other.

connecting ideas within and between sentences

albeit; also includes; although; apart from; because; because of this; before; better/worse; by comparison; by contrast; despite this/the fact that; effective/ineffective; especially; even if; even though; for example; furthermore; greater/fewer; hence; however; if ... then ...; in other respects; in particular; in spite of this; it follows that; more/less; most importantly; nevertheless; on the other hand; regardless; the effect of; therefore; thus; when ... then; whereas; while; with regard/s to

example – evaluating Bessie Smith's 'Backwater Blues' in relation to artistic intent (performance)

Bessie Smith's 'Backwater Blues' **is a highly effective** performance of a blues song. Smith uses her powerful voice to express the sorrow of the lyrics. Like many blues vocalists, she uses dynamic contrast to emphasise the lyrics, with the repeated phrase of each verse often a little quieter. **Furthermore,** Smith sings using a typical blues style of sliding between notes.

The performance **also includes** other features commonly heard in blues songs. **For example,** piano improvisation with contrasting rhythmic and melodic elements is used for each verse. Like the vocal melody, these instrumental fillers are based on the blues scale. The fillers are also a response to the singer's 'call', demonstrating the call and response pattern incorporated into many blues performances.

Most importantly, the melody harmonises with the twelve-bar blues chord progression, which is used in varying ways for each verse of the song. **While** at times a blues note clashes with a chordal note, this adds to the blues flavour. **Therefore, an evaluation of** Bessie Smith's performance of 'Backwater Blues' **shows that it convincingly demonstrates the** common features of a blues song.

example – evaluating exercise as a means of weight loss (process)

There is no doubt that exercise **has many** health **benefits, including** increased strength, fitness and mental wellbeing. Exercise as a means to weight loss, **however, may not be the best approach. While** aerobic exercise does burn kilojoules, **it takes** significant time and effort to make any real difference. **For example,** it would take a 7-km run or 90-minute walk to burn off 100 g of chocolate (2200 kJ or 500 calories). Most people cannot or will not sustain the lengthy time and effort needed to use exercise as their main method of keeping weight off or losing weight. **Further, markedly increased** exercise **leads to** increased appetite.

Scientific studies **reinforce this, suggesting that the** largest driver behind obesity is not how sedentary people are, but how poor their diet is. Exercise **only results in significant** weight loss **if combined with** calorie restriction. **On the other hand,** those who exercise while restricting food intake are more likely to retain muscle and lose fat. **Also, many people still prefer** exercise to dieting **as it can be** a much more enjoyable method of preventing the onset of type 2 diabetes than dieting, even if it is not quite as efficient.

Thus, despite the emphasis on exercise as the key to weight loss in many advertising campaigns from big takeaway food companies such as Coca-Cola and KFC, exercise **is not the most effective** method of weight loss.

example – evaluating the Paleo diet (product)

The Paleo diet is an eating plan based on the foods that our ancestors ate between 2.5 million and 12,000 years ago, during a time known as the Paleolithic Period. It comprises foods that were hunted and gathered rather than cultivated. Modern advocates of the diet aim to return to the foods that human beings used to eat. **Before deciding if** the Paleo diet is for you, **consider its advantages and disadvantages.**

Even though the diet avoids refined and processed foods, **it can lack** calcium, vitamins and fibre. It is rich in fruit, vegetables and nuts, which are essential elements of a healthy diet. **However,** whole grains, dairy products and legumes are omitted from the diet, and these are important foods that humans have evolved to eat. The Paleo diet is meat-heavy, **although** if the meat is lean, moderate amounts of fat are consumed. Higher quantities of healthy omega-3 and monounsaturated fats are consumed by people on this diet, **and this is a further advantage.**

There are some health **benefits and these include** promoting the eating of whole, nutritious food. Better blood pressure control **is also an advantage. On the other hand**, the diet may result in lethargy, headaches and bad breath. **There is evidence to suggest that the** risk of certain diseases such as heart disease and diabetes can be reduced.

For many people who struggle to lose or maintain weight, the Paleo diet **is appealing as it can lead to** weight loss through appetite management. **It contributes to** a feeling of fullness **and** may, **therefore**, prevent overeating. **However,** the initial rapid weight loss experienced in the first few weeks may not be sustained. **Because** certain foods are banned or 'off limits', cravings for these foods may develop, leading to people overeating them, **and this is a significant disadvantage of** the Paleo diet.

connecting ideas within and between sentences

albeit; also includes; although; apart from; because; because of this; before; better/worse; by comparison; by contrast; despite this/the fact that; effective/ineffective; especially; even if; even though; for example; furthermore; greater/fewer; hence; however; if ... then ...; in other respects; in particular; in spite of this; it follows that; more/less; most importantly; nevertheless; on the other hand; regardless; the effect of; therefore; thus; when ... then; whereas; while; with regard/s to

sentence starters

... and this is a further/significant advantage/disadvantage of ...
... and this is a good feature of the design.
... can improve ...
... convincingly demonstrates ...
... detracts from the overall appearance/performance of/by ...
... evokes a feeling of ... on the one hand, mixed with feelings of ... on the other.
... have emerged in an effort to address the disadvantages of ...
..., however, may not be the best approach.
... is a highly effective ...
... is also an advantage/disadvantage.
... is also damaging to ...
... is more appropriate/sustainable/aesthetically appealing, etc. than ...
... is/was particularly effective because ...
... is/would have been more appealing/better quality/more suited to the purpose than ...
... only results in significant ... if combined with ...
... reinforce this, suggesting that the ...
... would have been better, and this is noted for next time.
Also, many people still prefer ... as it can be ...
Because ..., ..., and this is a significant disadvantage of ...
Before deciding if ..., consider its advantages and disadvantages.
Even though ..., it can lack ...
Even though parts of ... are weak, the overall effect is stunning/impressive/memorable/etc.
For many people who ..., ... is appealing as it can lead to/prevent ...
Further, markedly increased ... leads to ...
However, the appeal of the performance/artwork lies in the way the elements have been combined to make powerful statements.
It contributes to ... and, therefore, ...
It worked reasonably well when ...; however, ... was especially effective.
Next time it would be a good idea to ... instead of ...
The ... is pleasing to the eye because ...
The appeal of ... lies ...
The following criteria will be used to evaluate the product/performance:
The main problem with ... is that ...
The most outstanding performance was by ... as he/she/they ...
The worst feature/part of ... is ... because ...
There are, however, definite downsides.
There are some ... benefits and these include ...
There is evidence to suggest that the ...
There is no/some/little doubt that ... has many ... benefits, including ...
Therefore, an evaluation of ... shows that it convincingly demonstrates the ...
This has its ... advantages, as it does not require ...
Thus, despite the emphasis on ..., ... is not the most effective ...
To improve the effectiveness of ..., several changes need to be made, which include ...
When evaluating ..., it is clear why this is such a complex issue.
While..., it takes ...

example – evaluating primary sources such as diaries and letters

purpose: This document **is a firsthand account of** the bombings of Dresden as told by Dick Sheehy, who was a British prisoner of war (POW) in Dresden at the time of the bombings. **The account was written in** 1995 and published in a copy of *History Today*. **The purpose of** this document **is to** give a firsthand account of the bombings of Dresden. **It not only** tells of the night of the bombings **but also** goes into detail about the events that followed. The author gives an account of the physical and mental struggles that he went through as a result of the bombing.

origin: This article **has value in that it is** a firsthand account. The author **goes into great detail about** his experience, leaving the reader to draw their own conclusions about whether the bombings were justifiable. **The** document **gives evidence that supports** research into the emotional impact of the air raids.

value: Firsthand accounts of historical events such as diaries, memoirs and letters **are important for research.** They provide a snapshot of the moment and reflect opinions of the time. **Certainly,** personal accounts such as diary entries or letters **give the reader an insight into** the characters of the writers and the impact the events they are describing have on them. **Despite** the lack of credentials of the author, personal accounts **are considered to be** authoritative, **especially if** they are created at the time of the event rather than much later when they are more likely to be an account of what the writer remembers rather than necessarily what happened.

limitations: **This value, however, can also act as a limitation. Because** the article is a firsthand account, **there is a strong possibility that** the author has forgotten important details. Also, the author has written his account many years after the event, meaning his memories could have altered. He might, as a result of the mental impacts of the war, think that some things may have happened when in fact they did not.

Sometimes, the immersion in the moment **may mean that critical details are overlooked.** Documents that describe events of war may be subject to censorship and key details of the account erased. When the source was written, it was probably not intended for a large audience so may be candid or revealing – a good and bad thing. **These sources are unavoidably biased because they** reflect the viewpoint of one person moulded by opinions, prejudices and the social and cultural context of the time. The writer selects what to include and what to omit. **The account may not be a true recollection of** events **as** details can become blurred by the passage of time. Memoirs may be shaped by what has happened since the event, and views change with time.

* The source document is not included.

sentence starters

... are valuable and important for research.
... goes into great detail about ...
... has value in that it is ...
... is a firsthand account of ...
Because ..., there is a strong possibility that ...
Certainly, ... give/s the reader an insight into ...
Despite ..., ... is/are considered to be ..., especially if ...
It not only ... but also ...
Sometimes, ... may mean that critical/crucial details are overlooked.
The ... gives evidence that supports ...
The account may not be a true recollection of ... as ...
The account was written in ...
The author gives an account of ...
The purpose of ... is to ...
These sources are unavoidably biased because they ...
This value, however, can also act as a limitation.

explaining

meaning: making an idea or situation plain or clear by giving reasons for both how and why something may have happened

things to know: An explanation includes the what (description), how (process or sequence) and why (justification or cause and effect). Therefore, the information elsewhere in this book about describing and justifying may also be useful when explaining. Many writers confuse the words affect (v) and effect (n), so make sure you understand their usage.

explaining how

example – explaining how river deltas form

River deltas **are** landforms **that occur where** rivers enter seas, oceans or lakes. **There are** three main shapes of deltas, **and each is determined by** the relationship between the river's flow and the amount of sediment transported by the river. Arcuate deltas are fan-shaped with the wider part of the fan facing the larger body of water. The Nile River in Egypt is an arcuate delta. The Mississippi River in the United States is an example of a bird's foot delta, which, as the name suggests, spreads out like the toes on a bird's foot. Less common are the cuspate deltas (such as Italy's River Tiber), which are shaped like teeth **because** the waves push the sediments outwards along the shore.

Not all rivers in the world have deltas, because certain conditions must exist to allow their formation. **The process begins with** a river carrying sediment or silt – material that has accumulated from surface run-off or riverbank erosion. **By the time a** river reaches its mouth, **it is** laden with sediment. As a river enters the end of its journey, its velocity decreases because of the low gradient and the large amount of sediment it carries. A delta forms where a river flows into a sea, ocean or lake that does not have strong tides or currents, **so** the sediment accumulates rather than being washed away into the open water. The sediment is called alluvium and builds up in layers, **usually after successive** floods. The delta extends the mouth of the river into the body of water it is entering. The low energy levels in the river **mean that the** river breaks up into several channels or distributaries and small islands form.

sentence starters

... are ... that occur where ...
... are most likely to occur when/where ...
... can lead to ...
... is the name given to ...
... leads to ...
... mean/s that the ...
... occur in a/no particular order ...
..., usually after successive ...
... usually occur/s when/if ...
After successive .../a significant amount of time ...
By the time a ..., it is ...
It is caused by ..., leading to ...
Other factors that contribute to this phenomenon are ...
The ... is ... which has/have ...
The changes also show/reflect ...
The factors that contribute to ... include ...
The first/next/final thing that happens is ...
The main effect of ...
The main reason ... occurs is ...
The process begins when/with ...
The reason for this situation is not clear; however, ...
The stages/steps involved are ...
There are ..., and each is determined by ...
There are several aspects to ..., particularly ...
There is a sequence behind ...
They are most likely to occur ... where/when/if ...
This happens because ...
This is because ...
This is followed by ...
This process/situation/event is called ... and starts with ...
To put it simply, ...

connecting ideas within and between sentences

also; also affect; and/and so; and this leads to; as; as a result of; because; by; cause; caused by; consequently; contributed to; due to; except/exception; for; for example/instance; for this reason; from this/these/that; generally; hence; if ... then; in addition; it follows that; now that; provided that; resulting in; results from/in; this is how/why; since; so; so that; such as; the effect of; the reason for; then; therefore; thus; unless; when; when ... then; while

example – explaining why the world has time zones

The world **is** divided into time zones **that have** specific times with different places on earth having different times. In the 1800s scientists calculated that there are twenty-four time zones. **Because of the** spherical shape of the earth, the distance between time zones at the equator is approximately 1600 km and at the poles is 0 km. There are two important lines of longitude or meridians: the prime meridian that is fixed from the Greenwich Observatory just south of London and the International Date Line (IDL) that runs through the Pacific Ocean.

The twenty-four time zones are distributed according to longitude, with every 15° roughly equivalent to one hour. **The reason for this is the** earth rotates once on an imaginary line or axis every 24 hours. One complete rotation of the earth is 360°, **so** by dividing this by 24 hours, it takes about one hour for the earth to rotate through 15°. Time zone boundaries are not always straight and tend to follow natural and/or political boundaries. **This ensures that** differences in time within countries cause minimal disruption.

Everyone on earth has the same pattern of sunrise and sunset, **so** wherever you are on the globe, noon is the middle of the day and midnight is the middle of the night. The time at the IDL is 12 hours behind Greenwich when travelling in a westerly direction and 12 hours ahead when travelling in an easterly direction. **This means that there is a** full day's difference in time immediately either side of the International Date Line. Travellers lose a day **when** going from the United States to Australia and gain a day **when** travelling in the other direction between the two countries.

sentence starters

... and this contributes to ...
... are also affected, and this leads to ...
... are caused by ...
... are usually caused when/by ...
... because ..., and so ...
... exist because ...
... has resulted in ...
... has several/multiple causes, which include ...
... has/have happened because ...
... is like this because ...
... occur rarely/frequently/occasionally/on a regular basis because ...
... will also affect ...
A similar outcome results from ...
As ..., it ...
As a result of ..., ... occurs ...
As a result of ..., several unforeseen events have occurred, including ...
Because of the ...
For that reason, ...
If ... were to change, then ... would happen.
It is also likely to cause ...
The ... is ... that have ...
The current situation exists because ...
The main effect/s of ... is/are ...
The main reason ... occur/s is/are ...
The process of ... is caused by ...
The reason for this is the ...
The resulting ...
There are ... main effects of ...
There are several reasons for ... including ...
This ensures that ...
This means that there is a ...

connecting ideas within and between sentences

also; also affect; and/and so; and this leads to; as; as a result of; because; by; cause; caused by; consequently; contributed to; due to; except/exception; for; for example/instance; for this reason; from this/these/that; generally; hence; if ... then; in addition; it follows that; now that; provided that; resulting in; results from/in; this is how/why; since; so; so that; such as; the effect of; the reason for; then; therefore; thus; unless; when; when ... then; while

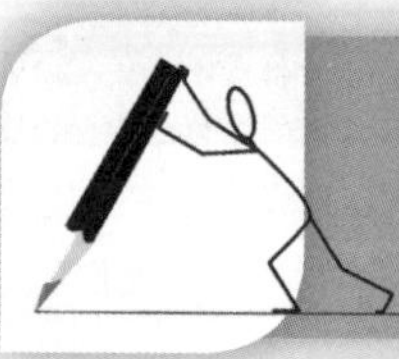

generalising

meaning: developing a broad statement that seems to be true in most situations or for most people; this does not include evidence or examples

things to know: Generalising is a useful skill because decisions can be made and actions undertaken based on things that people or situations have in common. Extreme generalising can lead to stereotyping, which may lead to prejudice and discrimination. Be careful to avoid making broad, sweeping statements when generalising. Use the lower intensity modal verbs (see page 66)

example – generalising about whether punctuation matters

Punctuation refers to those pesky little marks – **many of** them smaller than a pinhead – that give us so much trouble when we write. More and more mistakes are seen today, even on professionally produced written signs. Language is changing and evolving, so should punctuation change too? **Generally speaking,** we need to know when it matters and when it doesn't and be confident enough to use punctuation correctly.

In essence, punctuation **gives** meaning to language. Using it in the wrong place or not using it at all can have consequences. Sentences are the basis of all meaning, especially in written text, and if incorrectly punctuated, they might not make sense. Without punctuation, or correct punctuation, texts are difficult and slow to read, and this is inefficient. **Most people would agree that** correct punctuation is especially important when the writer and reader are not in the same place because there is no opportunity to make things clear.

In the vast majority of cases, writing that others will see needs to be correctly punctuated. This is because it is important to clearly and concisely communicate in all workplace settings. Harsh judgements can be made of us, especially in the workplace, if we make punctuation errors. Employers **may be reluctant to** give jobs to prospective employees if their writing is poorly constructed and punctuated.

With the advent of digital communications such as text messages, where the language is similar to speech, the question arises: is it necessary to punctuate these in the same way as writing? **Consensus among** language purists **is that** text messaging is causing standards to slip, and if punctuation does not matter as much today, then it could be spelling next! Could it be that **many of** the people who claim that punctuation does not matter are not very good at it themselves?

sentence starters

... has/have the same general idea/s as ...
... have a number of factors in common and these include ...
... is a broad statement that encompasses the essential elements of ...
... is a key factor in ...
... is more usual than ...
... is nowhere more evident than ...
... may be reluctant to ...
An examination of the data reveals several generalisations and these are as follows: ...
Another factor that ... have in common is that ...
Consensus among ... is that ... is/are ...
For the most part, ...
From the evidence, it is possible to suggest the following generalisation/s:
Generally speaking, ...
Generally speaking, several broad trends have emerged, which have contributed to ...
However, broadly speaking ...
However, there is certainly widespread agreement among members of society that considering ...
In a more general way, the ideas can be represented like this: ...
In essence, ... gives ...
In the usual course of events ...
In the (vast) majority of cases ...
In this instance, the general rule of ... is significant.
More general trends appear in the longer rather than the shorter term.
Most people would agree that ...
Nowadays, they will generally ...
The consensus among ... language purists seems to be that ...
The following photographs capture the essence of the topic.
The following summary captures the essence of the problem/situation/character's motives:
The general characteristics of ... are ...
The principle of ... can be applied to ...
The vast majority of ...
There are anomalies; however, a general pattern emerges, which is ...
There are exceptions to the general rule/trend, although, for the most part, it is relevant/ evident/significant ...
There are exceptions to the idea that ...
There are exceptions to this ... However, this of itself is ...
They are more/less likely to be ...
This includes considering ...
To summarise, then, ...
To summarise, then, the following generalisations are apparent.
While ..., a number of general statements can be made about ...
While there are exceptions to the rule, for the most part ... applies.

connecting ideas within and between sentences

as likely as not; broadly speaking; centrally; characteristically; commonly; essentially; for the most part; general/generally; in common; in general; in most/a large number of cases; in the main; likely; mainly; more likely than not; more often than not; most; most often; mostly; normally; often; on average; on the whole; primarily; quintessential/quintessentially; reasonably (assumed); regularly; suggested; typically; usually; widespread

inferring

meaning: using what is provided to make meaning or arrive at an answer or conclusion; uncovering the answer, even if it is not directly stated, using evidence and reasoning

things to know: Inference involves combining what you see (in words, tables or visual images) with what you know to generate meaning or understanding. It follows that inferences based on the same set of facts may vary from one person to another if their knowledge of the situation is different. Background knowledge is key to making valid inferences. These can be adequately supported by the information in the text, whereas invalid inferences cannot be supported by the information in the text. Invalid inferences stray too far from the text.

example – inferring from poetry

The first verse tells of the letter the writer wrote to Clancy. **It can be inferred that** he does not know Clancy's whereabouts now, **so** sends it to the place where he last remembers seeing Clancy. This place is the Lachlan River, which is part of the overflow of the Murrumbidgee River in the central west of New South Wales. The Lachlan River is one of the rivers in Australia that only flows after periods of heavy rain. **Even though** this region covers a large area of Australia, **it can be assumed that** the writer is hoping that someone will know Clancy and give him the letter.

The most likely inference to be made from what the reader is told in Verse Five **is that** the city is an unpleasant place to live and work. **Despite the fact** that Australia is sunny much of the time, the rays of sunshine do not reach the writer's office. He and others are engulfed by the smells and dirt of the city. In the final verse, the writer reflects on his life and compares it with Clancy's. **The reader can infer that** he is dissatisfied with his own lifestyle and envies what Clancy has – **so much so**, that he'd like to change places with him. **However**, Clancy would not like working in the office, **especially** work that involved keeping track of transactions.

Based on *Clancy of the Overflow* by AB 'Banjo' Paterson (1889).

sentence starters

... are commonly understood to mean ..., whereas ...
... is especially significant for the insight it provides into ...
... reveal/s a great deal about the topic, especially ...
...; therefore, a plausible inference is ...
A number of inferences are possible when viewing/reading/listening to this (text).
A viewer can make several inferences from ...
Another inference that can be made is that the image is ...
Even though ..., it can be assumed that ...
Even though it is not directly stated, it is apparent that ...
Even though there are ...
For this reason, it could be assumed that ...
From this data, it can be clearly inferred that ...
Given ..., it is most likely that ...
Hence, it is likely that ...
However, my interpretation is ...
I also know that ...
I think the first inference is more likely to be correct.
In addition, ... allows/permits/indicates/supports ...
In addition, it is likely that ... is reflecting on the ...
It appears that ...
It can be inferred that the relationship between ... and ... is ...
It could/can be (logically) inferred that ... so ...
It is likely that ... because ...
It is reasonable to assume that there are ...
It/they provide/s a valuable insight into ...
One/Another inference that can be made is that ... is reflecting on the ...
The fact that ... supports this inference.
The most likely inference to be made from what the reader is told in ... is that ...
The photograph shows a ...
The reader can infer that ...
The (text) provides a valuable insight into/allows us to infer that ...
The (text) states/reveals/shows ..., and this means ...
Therefore, the ... elements ... indicate ...
Therefore, the (text) means/indicates ...
They provide a valuable insight into ...
This (text) successfully conveys several meanings, each of which ...
While this would ..., it is most likely that ...

connecting ideas within and between sentences

although; apparently; appears; as a result of; associated with; because; consequently; despite (the fact); due to; especially; even though; evidently; for example; hence; however; if ... then; in addition; in other words; it appears; it is clear; it means that; might mean; provide; since; so; so much so; specifically; therefore; this can; this is; unless; whereas

interpreting

meaning: drawing meaning from information presented in various ways, using knowledge and understanding; demonstrating a unique understanding of a text from the arts and using that to create a product or performance

things to know: An interpretation often starts with a description of what is being interpreted and a discussion of the purpose of the information. It then explains the meaning and importance of different parts of the text and how they interact. The conclusion might include how well or clearly the information achieves its purpose and how it might be used to inform decisions.

example – interpreting a historical account of the Black Death

The Black Death, or bubonic plague, was a disease that decimated the population of Europe in the 14th century. It was at its worst between 1347 and 1351. **It is believed to have** come from Asia via the Silk Road along which traders travelled, bringing goods to Europe. **A number of firsthand accounts survive that give us insights into not only** the disease itself **but also** the changes to the social structure that the disease brought about. **One such account was written in a** chronicle at the cathedral priory of Rochester between 1314 and 1350.

The 'great mortality' **refers to the** millions of deaths that occurred from the disease, which is particularly virulent and thought to be spread by fleas carried by rats. **Because** the conditions of the day were unsanitary by today's standards, rats were everywhere, and **this meant that** there were many opportunities for the disease to spread.

According to the text, 'more than a third of the men, women and children' died from the disease, **and this led to** severe shortages of labourers to do the work, **especially** the work required by the lords of the manors. The feudal system of the time meant that the lords relied on the peasants and serfs. **Even though** lords had money and possessions, they were unable to find enough people to do their work. This gave the workers more power.

People did not have the means to dispose of dead bodies quickly or hygienically enough. Survivors were kept busy carrying the bodies of the plague victims, including children, for burial. **As** the people were dying faster than they could be buried, **this suggests that** the conditions in the graveyards were dreadful. Individual graves were not possible so bodies were thrown 'into mass graves, from which arose such a stink that it was barely possible for anyone to go past a churchyard'.

sentence starters

... and this led to ..., especially ...
... can be interpreted to mean that ...
... has several possible interpretations; however, ...
... is based on ...
... reveals a great deal about the character/situation/problem/topic.
A common but incorrect interpretation is ...
A number of firsthand accounts survive that give us insights into not only ... but also ...
According to ..., and this led to ...
As ..., this suggests that ...
Because ..., meaning is constructed in this (text) through the use of ...
Even though it is not directly admitted to, ...
From ..., a great deal can be understood, especially the ...
From the outset, it is clear that ...
However, if ..., then ...
It is believed to have ...
It is reasonable to assume that ...
It is unclear what ... means, but a plausible explanation is ...
Its ... are simple but its messages profound.
Looking more closely at ..., we can see that ...
My interpretation of ... is supported by ...
One such account was written in a ...
Smith (2016) stated ..., and this directly supports the findings of Jones (2014), who noted ...
The ... provides a valuable insight into ...
The ... refers to the ...
The ... represent/s ...
The use of ... further enhances ...
There are several interpretations of ...; however, the most common one is ...
There are several interpretations of the same event, but the most common one/most popular is ...
These messages are conveyed through the use of the ...
This could mean that ..., if we are prepared to ...
This further contributes to the message that the ...
This is because the expression ... means it is very clear ...
This means that ...
This provides a valuable insight into/indicates a sense of ...
This suggests that ... and ...
Through this simple tale, we see that ...
While ... is commonly understood to mean ..., I think it means ...

connecting ideas within and between sentences

according to; after; alternate/alternatively; although; and reveal; as; as a result; as then; at the same time; because; by contrast; clearly; consequently; despite; due to; especially; even though; evidently; far from; for example/instance; furthermore; hence; however; in addition; in other words; in particular; in that respect; instead of; it appears; it is clear; it is evident; it means that; may mean that; might mean; nevertheless; overall; refers to; results; revealed by; shows; since; such; that is; the reasons for; therefore; this is how; this is why; this meant that; whereas; while

justifying

meaning: showing or proving that an answer, argument, response, statement, conclusion or idea about something is reasonable or necessary by giving sound, logical and plausible reasons or evidence for it; answers the question 'why?'

things to know: A complete justification describes the decision and then provides reasons for that decision. It answers the question 'why?'. It explains why you support a course of action or have a particular belief. Your justification may be the result of inductive or deductive thinking.

example – justifying the decision to cancel your credit card

Credit in business is the ability of the customer to obtain goods and services before payment, based on the trust and expectation that the amount owing will be paid at some future date. Credit is not a new concept, but the ability to get credit in recent times has been made much easier by credit cards. The 'live now, pay later' philosophy rarely happens without the consumer having to pay interest. In an effort to encourage consumers to buy goods and services, some businesses offer a period of time when no interest is charged. **However**, when interest is charged after the 'interest-free period', it can be very high. **Needless to say,** many people get into financial difficulty, **so** for them **it may be** time to cancel their credit cards.

There are a number of reasons for this recommendation. Without a credit card, you only spend within your means. Spending is more mindful and saving is possible. The decision to buy or not buy something is easy; if you cannot afford it, you do not buy it. With a credit card, debts can increase beyond control, a situation made much worse when high rates of interest are added to the debt when the whole amount is not paid off by the due date. Late payment fees and other charges increase debt. **Consequently, it would seem better for** many of us to hand in our credit cards.

Debt can be very stressful and cause personal problems. Life is much easier without worrying debt. A credit card allows us to spend beyond our capacity to earn, **and this is another reason** to cancel the piece of plastic. **There is, therefore, no doubt that** for some people a credit card **is not a good idea**. Cancelling the card **is an intelligent response to the problem of** debt levels that are out of control.

sentence starters

... and this can lead to ...
... and this is a/another reason ...
... have some other traits that support the conclusion that ...
... is a better option because ...
... is a good idea because ...
... is a necessary/reasonable course of action because/given ...
... is a valid recommendation/suggestion based on ...
... is well supported by the evidence, which states that ...
... shows/is an intelligent response to the problem/issue/topic of ...
... will prove to be the best decision in the long term because ...
Another feature that substantiates ...
Another reason for this inclusion/decision is ...
Circumstances suggest the following course of action because ...
Consequently, it would seem better to/for ...
Despite the fact that there have been ...
Firstly/Secondly/Thirdly/Finally, ... and this is a reason ...
For now, ... is a better choice because ...
It is fact rather than opinion that supports the decision of ...
It is well supported by evidence ..., which states that ...
Needless to say, ..., so ... it may be ...
On balance, the evidence supports the view/opinion/decision that ...
Records show that ... were ... and ...
The argument is supported by ...
The best decision/course of action is ... because ...
The decision to/by ... is an effective response, therefore, to changing circumstances.
The reasons that support the choice of ... are solid and based on factual evidence.
The weight of evidence suggests that ...
There are no valid reasons to support this conclusion.
There are several/many/a number of reasons for this recommendation/recommended action/decision/conclusion.
There are several/many/a number of reasons why this is a far-sighted response to ...
There is, therefore, no/some/much doubt that ... is/is not a good idea.
These reasons are solid and based on factual evidence that proves that ...

connecting ideas within and between sentences

adds weight to; although; and this will/can lead to; as; as a result; because; better/worse; confirm/confirms; consequently; corroborate/corroborates; definitely; even though; greater/fewer; hence; however; in order for/to; in spite of; in this situation; is conclusive/inconclusive; is preferred because; more than/less than; needless to say; produce/produces; prove/proves; reinforce/reinforces; show/shows; so; substantiate/substantiates; support/supports; therefore; under the circumstances; validate/validates; will ensure

persuading

meaning: attempting to convince someone to believe an idea or opinion or to accept a point of view and act upon it

things to know: Persuasive writing can be less formal than argument or exposition. It is likely to contain the writer's point of view, and they may draw on personal experience to substantiate this view; hence, personal pronouns are used. Techniques such as rhetoric, repetition, high modality, rule of three and including the reader are used. Good persuasive writers use a technique similar to one used in a debate. To strengthen an argument, the writer acknowledges an opposing argument and refutes it. For example, opponents of legalising marijuana claim that usage will increase if the substance is made legal. However, countries where the drug is legal have reported no increase in its use.

example – persuading that graffiti is an eyesore

Looking out of the train recently on my journey into the centre of the city, my eyes were assaulted by endless images of graffiti defacing the walls of buildings, bridges, railway embankments and even people's homes. **There is no doubt in my mind that** graffiti is an eyesore and should be removed immediately.

There are those who claim that graffiti is artistic and enhances the built environment. **This might be the case if** everyone were a Banksy. **The fact is that anyone can** buy spray paint and mark their territory with words and images that are as ugly as they are offensive. **Do I hear you say that** graffiti is artistic and spectacular murals have been created by artists who can actually paint? **This may be so, but** these quality pieces are few and far between. Most graffiti makes urban areas look as though they are in decline and a haven for crime and drug dealers and users.

Some argue that graffiti improves the appearance of the concrete jungle that is dominated by dull, grey concrete walls. **However**, people have not asked for the walls of their property to be smeared with paint. Most people want the value of their property to go up, not down, and unattractive graffiti lowers the value of property. **To those people who say that** graffiti is a means of expressing points of view about important issues, **I say** write a letter to the editor instead. **So, let's** clean up **our** urban environments **and** remove this unattractive paintwork immediately.

sentence starters

... has/have been vehemently opposed to ...
... it is up to us to ...
... (State point of view). There are several convincing arguments to support this point of view.
... while important, is not a complete/appropriate/valid solution to ...
A major appeal of ...
Advocates of ... argue that ..., but ...
All the evidence points conclusively to ...
As an added bonus, ...
Do I hear you say that ...?
Firstly, let us consider the argument that ... – easy to state but difficult to substantiate.
In recent years, however, there have been calls for ...
In recent years, opinion has become much more divided on the issue of ...
It is up to us to ...
It would appear that the issue of ... is quite straightforward; however, closer inspection reveals compelling arguments both for and against ...
It would be virtually impossible for anyone to make a decent case for ...
Not only are they ..., they ...
Nothing polarises opinion in quite the same way as the issue of ...
One of the main advantages/disadvantages of ...
One way to address ... is ...
Opponents of ... claim ..., however, ...
So, let's ... our ... and ...
Some argue that ...
Some people claim that ...
The decision is an easy one.
The fact is that anyone can ...
The issue of ... is highly controversial because ...
There are those who claim that ...
There is no/little/a great deal (of) doubt (in my mind) that ...
There is strong evidence to support ...
This may be so, but ...
This might be the case if ...
This would be a terrible/wonderful decision for ...
To those people who say that ..., I say ...
While there are several convincing arguments that support this point of view, the balance of the argument is weighted in favour of ...

connecting ideas within and between sentences

absolutely; admittedly; allow; also (give); at one/another level; because; beyond doubt; clearly; despite/in spite (of); ends up as; even though; evidence suggests; extremely; far less/more; finally; furthermore; generally; hence; however; less/more; if ... then/we can ...; in addition; in conclusion; inevitable/inevitably; instead of; like/unlike; likely that; more difficult; moreover; much easier; need to; nevertheless; not only ... but also ...; obvious/obviously; of course; on the other hand; one reason for; only/not only; overall; particularly; rather than; similarly; so; such as; surely; therefore (it seems); this/that; thus; ultimately; undoubtedly; which could/could not; while; without (question); would/would not

predicting

meaning: suggesting what might happen or give an expected result based on the available information and what is known about a topic

things to know: Predictions are useful because they prompt us to think about what something might be like. They are not wild guesses. When making a prediction, take into account what has already happened or what is already known about a topic. Predictions are neither right nor wrong but must be justified based on sound knowledge. Predictions can be revised at any time as circumstances change. Longer-term predictions are more difficult to make than those in the short term.

example – predicting that by 2050, more people will work from home than work in institutions such as offices

For centuries, whether it was on a farm, in an office or in a factory, employees went to a place of work. They had designated hours, days off and holidays. **However**, the nature of work is changing. **Nowadays there are fewer** jobs in manufacturing **and more** in the service sector, and many of the latter can be done from home. **Based on current trends, which show that** an increasing number of people want to work from home and employers are agreeing to this, **it is likely that by** 2050, the vast majority of employees **will** work from home. **Nevertheless**, there will always be some jobs that require a face-to-face or physical presence, such as those in building and construction, hair and beauty, and hospitality and tourism sectors. **It is, therefore, highly unlikely that** everyone will work from home in 2050.

Technology **has allowed** many jobs to be done without an employee being physically present. **Nowhere is this more apparent than in the rise of** offshore call centres, where an enquiry about a telephone service in Australia can be resolved by a call centre operator in the Philippines. **As a result of** work becoming more specialised, it is necessary and now possible to tap into the skills of people from all over the world. Employers can attract employees from a wider workforce, helping them to address shortages of labour.

Another reason for this prediction is that people in the workforce today are very comfortable and competent with technology. They can solve their own problems or find someone online who can. This reduces the need to be in a place of work with support staff. It is likely that in a post-pandemic world, working from home will continue.

Working from home has become more popular and is increasing dramatically. **Studies show that** employees **cite** flexibility **as one of the main reasons** they like it so much. **Further evidence suggests that** more people would work from home if they could. **Another reason why the trend towards** working from home **will increase is linked to** concerns for the environment. There is no need for commuting, which costs time and money and adds to carbon emissions. Employers also benefit from this trend. Employees are often prepared to be paid less money for the flexibility of working from home, **so** the cost of wages is reduced.

sentence starters

... has allowed ...
... is probably going to be ...
..., therefore ... is likely to be/have ...
A further prediction can be made based on what would happen if ...
Another reason for the/this prediction is that ...
Another fact that validates the prediction is ...
Another reason why the trend towards ... will increase is linked to ...
As ... becomes ..., it is possible to ...
Based on current trends, which show that ..., it is likely that by ..., ... will ...
Based on this, I predict that ... will have much more/less ... than ...
Further evidence suggests that ...
Given that ..., then it is highly likely ... will be the ...
If this trend continues, then it is expected that ... will occur.
In the future, it is highly probable that ...
It is probable that the ... would be ...
It is, therefore, highly unlikely that ...
Nowadays there are fewer/more ... and more/fewer ...
Nowhere is this more apparent than in the rise of ...
One possible outcome/result/consequence of ... is likely to be ...
One prediction was that ... would have ...
Studies show that ... cite ... as one of the main reasons ...
The ... is a final reason it is likely ...
The outcome would almost certainly be similar/different, although there is likely to be less/more ...
The reason for this is ...
This is another point that lends weight to the prediction ... will ...
This is because ..., especially ...
This is crucial because of the ...

connecting ideas within and between sentences

alternatively; although; and so; and this leads to ...; as a result of ...; because; consequently; could result in; due to; even so; even though; for this reason; from this/these/that; hence; however; if; if ... then ...; in spite of this; it follows that; likely/unlikely; nevertheless; not only ... but also ...; probable/probably; provided that; resulting in; results; results from; since; so (that); such as; the reason for; then; therefore; thus; unless; when ... then ...; whereas; which means that; which would; while; would have; yet

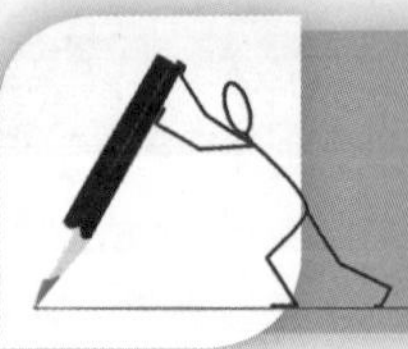

providing evidence

meaning: referring to sources, illustrations and other evidence about something to support the points being made

things to know: Providing evidence of a claim or point of view adds weight and validity to that point of view. Evidence can take many forms, from what one person thinks to facts and figures that lend weight to claims. It is important to ensure that any evidence used comes from a reliable, credible, current and unbiased source.

example – providing evidence that Genghis Khan was a savage, ruthless barbarian

Genghis Khan, a name that means 'universal ruler', was a 13th-century warrior. **As** the leader of the Mongolian tribes, which he united, he defeated great empires and occupied much of China. At its height, the Mongol Empire stretched from the Adriatic Sea in Europe to the Pacific coast of Asia, an area approximately the size of Africa. **Despite historical evidence to show that he was** a gifted military leader and an enlightened ruler, **his legacy has been dominated by** his reputation as a ferocious barbarian.

Genghis Khan's **name has become synonymous with** brutality, and history remembers him as a ruthless killer and savage monster. He was responsible for the massacre of millions of men, women and children in the territories he conquered. Usually, their throats were cut and they drowned in a sea of blood. Estimates put the number of deaths at about 40 million – twice as many as were slaughtered by Russian leader Stalin in the 20th century. **Historians also believe that** northern China lost two-thirds of its population during his rule. Passing through Kiev in 1246, Giovanni da Pian del Carpini recorded that he came across countless human skulls and bones.

The Mongolians, under the leadership of Genghis Khan, burned cities, used captured enemies as human shields, and enslaved survivors and forced them to live elsewhere; **furthermore**, if they did not surrender, they died. Persian historian Juvaini (c. 1250) **observed that** 'they [the Mongolians] came, they slew, they plundered and they departed'. **The** horrific **nature of the methods used to** kill their victims **provides evidence of** their savagery. Many victims had their backs broken or were suffocated. One particularly vile method was to pour molten silver into enemies' eyes and ears. 'Like hungry falcons attacking a flight of doves or raving wolves attacking sheep', recorded Persian historian Abdullah Wassaf in 1258, the Mongols showed no mercy. Genghis Khan's brutality was not limited to his enemies; he had no qualms about killing his half-brother after a hunting dispute.

* This example refers to sources and uses direct quotes without adding the source details. Normally, the source details are added after the direct quotes.

sentence starters

(Author, date) argues that ..., and this is supported by (author, date)
... and this has been used as another piece of evidence to support ...
... and this lends further weight to the idea that ...
... gathered her/his/their first piece of evidence from ...
... has enabled more links to be made between ...
... name has become synonymous with ...
... observed that ...
... published compelling evidence from ..., but because s/he/they was/were unable to explain how/why ..., her/his/their ideas were rejected by ...
... theory is now universally accepted as an explanation of ..., although nowadays it is ...
... who claim that the ... said that just because ..., was insufficient to explain or provide evidence for ...
A survey of ... found that ...
According to (author, date), who stated that ..., ... is valid/invalid.
An examination of the figures for ... creates further alarm/optimism/encouragement.
Analysis of the data suggests ...
As there are significant and alarming differences between ... and ..., the ... introduced ...
Despite historical evidence to show that she/he/they was/were ..., her/his/their legacy has been dominated by ...
Evidence for this existed in ...
Further evidence of the disparity exists in the ...
Historians also believe that ...
However, counterclaims state that the ...
Initially, it was thought that ...
Several authors/experts (author 1, date; author 2, date; author 3, date) are in agreement about ...
The ... evidence that ... collected gave further support to her/his/their theory.
The ... is double/triple/quadruple/half the rate of the ..., and this has been increasing over time.
The ... nature of the methods used to ... provides evidence of ...
The ... of ... compared with ...
The evidence collected allows the following observations to be made:
The evidence that ... gathered from ... is compelling proof of the ...
The figures for those in the ... have shown some improvement.
The final piece of evidence that ... used to support ... was based on the ...
There are significant differences between the ...
There are two schools of thought among ..., and these are that ...
There is evidence from ... that ...
These are staggering figures, given that the ...
This has not been the case with figures for ...
This theory was partially corroborated by ...
This/these argument/s is/are confirmed by several authors including (author, date), who states that ...
To prove this, she/he/they ...
Today, the bulk of evidence supports the ..., and most ... are in agreement about this.

connecting ideas within and between sentences

according to; almost; also; although; approximately; as; as well as; based on; because; believed; but; case in point; clearly; closely; confirmed by; contradicts; corroborates; despite; evident/evidently; examine/examines; exists; for example/instance; for this reason; furthermore; however; illustrates; in addition to; in detail; indeed; indicates; initially; it is clear that; less/more than; like/unlike; means; moreover; namely; observed; refutes; reveals; shows; such as; suggest/s; support/s; through; to prove this;

quoting

meaning: repeating the exact words, usually by copying them out, that were written (or spoken) by another person

things to know: A quote provides evidence or authority for a point that the writer/speaker wants to make. It is important to always acknowledge where the statements used have come from. This is done by using quotation marks and acknowledging the source of the quote. Use quotes judiciously – that is, avoid using lengthy quotes as they often do not add to your writing. Punctuating quotes is tricky and can vary according to the style guidelines being followed. Be sure to revise the rules of punctuation when you introduce quotes. Note the use of direct quotes, indicated by either '...' or "..." (depending on style), and indirect quotes where the speech is reported and paraphrased rather than directly quoted. However, the source is still acknowledged for indirect quotes in the same way as with direct quotes. All sources cited in a piece of writing should be listed in a reference list at the end.

example – quoting evidence to support reasons for a recommendation

The weight of evidence suggests that the most important resolution **would be to** employ a teacher with expert basketball coaching skills at our school. This teacher would promote basketball in the school and provide more opportunity for training and games, increasing the skill level of the students. **As** Rock (2018) **confirms,** 'in 98% of cases it was apparent that the most important factor in the facilitation of change in the practices and values of sport is people'. Currently, although staff are supportive of basketball, there are no expert basketball coaches at our school. **Regardless of** a school's resources and facilities, **in order for** a sport to become significant in any school, **there needs to be** at least one passionate and skilled staff member to ensure success (Me, 2014).

As a result of employing a basketball specialist at the school, a second resolution could be to offer a Sporting Excellence Program for basketball. This would consequently attract skilled players to our school and overcome the barrier of touch football, tennis and surfing dominating our school sporting culture. **This is supported by** Ement (2016)**, who concluded that** the ability to provide students with expert training and regular participation was key to a sport's success. Once students begin to experience success at interschool competitions, more students will become interested. **As** Zee (2015) **declares,** 'winning quickly cultivates popularity'.

As well as increasing the level of expertise among students, having a Sporting Excellence Program for basketball **would also produce** a 'critical mass' of students wanting to play at lunchtimes. This would give students greater opportunities to play basketball for recreational purposes, hence building the momentum of participation among students.

* A piece of writing such as this should include a correctly formatted bibliography or reference list at the end. Also, when quoting material directly, the citation needs to include the specific page number or other identifier such as paragraph number for online material with no page numbers.

sentence starters

... agrees/disagrees with this, ...
... comes to the conclusion that ...
... contradicts the commonly held beliefs that ...
... is in full agreement about ...
... makes it very clear that ...
... offers a well-considered solution to ...
... offers an alternative explanation for ...
... pleads the case for ...
... point out ...
... proposes a more viable solution to ...
... provided this insight, ...
... puts forward the view that ...
... rejects the evidence/all other alternatives that ...
... reported/s the following findings:
... repudiates the arguments that ...
... urges the reader to ...
According to ...
As ... confirms/declares/reports, ...
As a result of ...
As well as increasing/decreasing ..., ... would also produce ...
Further evidence that ...
However, others argue that despite ..., ... is not the ...
Instead, ... declared that ...
Regardless of ..., in order for ..., there needs to be ...
Smith (year) is in total agreement/disagreement with Jones (year) when ...
The problem with, ... argued, is/was ...
The weight of evidence suggests that the most important ... would be to ...
There is evidence of ...
This is supported by ..., who concluded that ...
This supports ...'s assertion that ...

connecting ideas within and between sentences

admit/ted/s; admonish/ed/es; argue/d/s; assert/ed/s; claim/ed/s; conclude/d/s; concur/red/s (with); confirm/ed/s; declare/d/s; estimate/d/s; explain/ed/s in some/more detail; indicate/d/s; stress/ed/es the point; suggest/ed/s; vehemently deny/ied/s; warns

recommending

meaning: suggesting a course of action for consideration by others and a procedure or set of instructions for enacting the action; providing reasons (usually the findings of an investigation or research) in favour of a suggestion

things to know: Recommendations usually provide reasons for actions linked to the findings of an investigation or research. In this respect, they can be similar to justifications. They can also suggest a process or method, in the form of a procedure or set of instructions, by which recommendations can be carried out. Recommending is not a standalone skill and may require other skills to be demonstrated, such as explaining, comparing, analysing and justifying.

recommending how

example – recommending how water should be conserved in Australia

Even though Australia is one of the driest continents, Australians are among the highest consumers of water on earth. Compared with other places, Australia's total rainfall is small, and as frequent droughts prove, the supply is unreliable. Saving fresh water is vital because only 1% of the world's fresh water is available for drinking.

A lot of water is wasted waiting for running tap water to turn cold or hot, **so follow this good piece of advice.** Keep a bottle of tap water in the fridge for drinking **so** you don't have to wait until the water turns cold. Use the half-flush on the toilet. For old toilets, put pebbles or bricks in the cistern **because** this decreases the amount of water used. Ensure that dishwashers and washing machines operate with a full load. **If possible,** install a water tank to catch rainwater.

Several water-saving **measures can be implemented in the** garden. Planting natives, which require less water, will create a 'waterwise garden'. **It is further recommended to** keep the grass longer as it shades the soil and reduces evaporation. Avoid overwatering the lawn because grass can be trained to send its roots deeper to search for water. **If you have** a pool or spa, **it is worthwhile** covering them to minimise evaporation.

All these measures comprise an intelligent response to the problem of water shortages in Australia.

sentence starters (process/procedure/instructions)

... is a summary of the recommendations presented in the report.
... is another important recommendation for ...
... is every bit as important as ...
... is paramount, and it is therefore recommended ...
..., so follow this good piece of advice.
...; therefore, in the future it is proposed that ...
All these measures comprise an intelligent response to the problem of ...
Based on the analysis of the situation, the following recommendations have emerged:
Based on the findings, the following recommendations are put forward for discussion:
Becoming familiar with ... is also recommended, and it is advisable to ...
Failure to follow these recommendations could have serious ramifications.
For the future, it is recommended that ...
Having examined the evidence available, it is clear that ... is the best recommendation for ...
However, if ..., it is strongly recommended ...
I confidently recommend the following changes:
If the following recommendation/s is/are implemented, then the problem should be solved.
If you have ..., it is worthwhile ...
In light of all the available data, the proposed recommendation is ...
In spite of ..., the best solution is ...
It is advisable to use ... rather than ..., even though ...
It is further recommended to ...
It is reasonable to conclude that ...; therefore, it is recommended that the ...
It is recommended that people know this and also spend time ...
It is, therefore, advisable to propose that ...
It would appear reasonable to conclude that ..., and therefore recommend ...
My recommendation, after looking at all the evidence, is to ...
Several ... measures can be implemented in the ...
The following recommendations, listed in order of priority, are put forward for consideration.
There are a couple of recommendations from which to choose.
There are a number of recommendations that all those ... should implement before ...
There are no guarantees that these recommendations will work; however, to do nothing may see the situation worsen.
These circumstances suggest that ... is vital ..., and it is recommended that some ... are adopted.
To achieve the goal of ..., it is suggested ...
To avoid ..., it is necessary to ...

connecting ideas within and between sentences

accordingly; additionally; all things considered; as a result; because; consequently; could/should/would; especially; even though; finally; hence; however; if possible; if ... then; in summary; in the end; in the final instance; is desirable; is favoured; is necessary; is recommended; is valid; moreover; on balance; so; sometimes; then; therefore; these include; thus; to act upon; to conclude; to summarise, then; we can conclude; we can recommend; while; will achieve

recommending why

example — recommending why water should be conserved in Australia

Even though Australia is one of the driest continents, Australians are among the highest consumers of water on earth. Compared with other places Australia's total rainfall is small, and as frequent droughts prove, the supply is unreliable. Saving fresh water is vital because only 1% of the world's fresh water is available for drinking.

The main reason water **must be** conserved **is because it is** finite and we do not have an endless supply. The world's population is increasing rapidly, needing more food and water. **While** we can survive for a couple of weeks without food, it is impossible to survive for more than a couple of days without water. Water is literally life.

Climate change **has led to a situation where** rainfall is less in some parts of the world and more unpredictable. Lower figures than long-term averages are being recorded. A hotter planet means a greater demand for water. Water is integral to the preservation of the environment, **especially** ecosystems and endangered species.

Conserving water **makes sound economic sense as it saves money**. Water is not free; it is expensive to move and process water and pay for the energy to do these things. Using water more carefully, and reducing the amount we use, reduces our carbon footprint by reducing pollution and using less energy.

There is no doubt, then, that measures to conserve water **must be adopted by** everyone **if we are to have** enough of this precious commodity for the future.

sentence starters (reasons)

... has led to a situation where ...
... is a better option because ...
... is a good idea because ...
... is a reasonable/necessary/desirable/timely course of action because ...
... is a valid recommendation/suggestion based on ...
... is well supported by evidence, which states that ...
... it is critical to ... to avoid problems, some of which can be severe.
... makes sound economic sense as it saves money.
... recommended that a/an ... be developed immediately.
... shows an intelligent response to the problem/issue/topic of ...
... will ensure that ..., such as ... is/are minimal.
... will prove to be the best recommendation in the long term because ...
A final reason for the urgency of enacting this recommendation is ...
All things considered, ... is an advisable course of action. It just makes good sense.
Another reason for (recommendation) is that it is not always possible to ...
Circumstances support the following course of action because ...
Consequently, it would seem better to ... because ...
Finally, ... is more appealing when ...
For now, ... is the better choice because ...
Having examined the evidence available, it is clear that ... is the best recommendation for ...
It is a relatively simple way of ...
Of further concern is the fact that the ...
On balance, the evidence supports the view/opinion/decision that ...
One of the few things that studies consistently agree upon is ...
Some of the reasons for this recommendation are:
The decision to ... is a good one as it is ...
The facts that support the recommendation include ...
The main reason ... must be ... is because it is ...
The main reason that ... is a suitable suggestion is ...
The reasons that support the choice of Recommendation A are solid and based on factual evidence.
The recommendation to ... is an effective response to changing circumstances.
The weight of evidence would suggest that ...
There are a number of reasons ... contribute/s to ...
There are several/many reasons for this recommendation/recommended action/decision, including ...
There is no doubt that the ... are ... and leave ...
There is no doubt, then, that measures to ... must be adopted by ... if we are to have ...
There is therefore no/some/much/little doubt that the ... are ... and leave ...

connecting ideas within and between sentences

accordingly; additionally; all things considered; as a result; because; consequently; could/should/would; especially; even though; finally; hence; however; if possible; if ... then; in summary; in the end; in the final instance; is desirable; is favoured; is necessary; is recommended; is valid; moreover; on balance; so; sometimes; then; therefore; these include; thus; to act upon; to conclude; to summarise, then; we can conclude; we can recommend; while; will achieve

reflecting

meaning: responding in a personal way, by thinking deeply and carefully, to something such as an issue, an image, a product or an action by making a personal connection with the information or ideas that appear

things to know: Reflection is personal and requires serious thought and consideration. It deepens learning and understanding. Use of the personal pronouns 'I', 'me' and 'my' is acceptable in reflective writing because personal responses are encouraged and respected. Language choices may be more informal than with other forms of writing but should still respect the reader.

example – reflecting on Bill and Melinda Gates's philanthropic work

Bill Gates, co-founder of Microsoft, and his wife, Melinda, manage the Gates Foundation, the world's largest private charity. Bill is one of the richest men in the world with a net worth of over 100 billion US dollars (2019), and **despite** donations of billions of dollars to charitable organisations, his money continues to grow. **I cannot comprehend the** amount of money that these figures represent – **it is certainly beyond the realms of anything I can** expect to experience.

So, why do some extremely wealthy people become philanthropists and work very hard to give away the money that they have spent their lives making? **Surely, it is not possible to** spend billions of dollars unless your plan is to go into outer space on a regular basis. This amount of money cannot be spent by an individual. Bill and Melinda Gates believe that once you've taken care of yourself and your family, the best use of wealth is to give it back to society. They both grew up in homes where it was instilled into them that the world should be left in a better place than they found it. The Gates Foundation supports organisations in over one hundred countries, including the United States, on such projects as combating the spread of malaria and eradicating polio.

I used to think that philanthropists just gave their money away in a rather random way. **This is not the case with** Bill Gates. He applies the same business management strategies to philanthropic work as he did when he managed Microsoft. Money is carefully distributed so that others can learn to help themselves rather than just rely on handouts. **Furthermore**, he says that philanthropic work is meaningful and fun. He particularly enjoys 'digging' behind the science of the Foundation's many projects.

Even though philanthropists often get recognition for their work in the form of honorary titles or degrees, **I do not think this is why the** Gateses do what they do. **Nor do I believe** they are looking to make more money for themselves through contacts that may give them economic advantages. **It is evident that** they are committed to improving the lives of millions of people around the world, **and for that they deserve** our admiration and respect.

Reference: Gates, B., & Gates, M. (2018, February 13). Our 2018 annual letter: 10 tough questions we get asked. GatesNotes. https://www.gatesnotes.com/2018-Annual-Letter?WT.mc_id=02_13_2018_02_AnnualLetter2018_BG-TW_&WT.tsrc=BGTW&linkId=47931674

sentence starters

... caused me to reflect on ... and to what extent I had been ...
... realised that, while this was helpful, it did not give ...
... thinks that being more ... would be beneficial and would ensure that ...
... were known to me, especially ...
Even though ..., I do not think this is why the ... Nor do I believe ...
Finally, I think it would also ...
Fortunately, I was able to correct the mistakes I made.
However, what disappoints me is that ...
I am full of admiration for ...
I am much more conscientious about ...
I am reasonably satisfied that my ... is ...
I cannot comprehend that/the ... – it is certainly beyond the realms of anything I can ...
I had ... but did not always ...
I had read that ... and had been ...
I have been/was concerned/not concerned about ..., although I always ...
I have heard them ...
I have witnessed other situations where ...
I learnt/have learnt from this that ...
I think that ... have ...
I think that the ...
I used to think that ... This is not the case with ...
I was not concerned about ..., although always ...
I would like to ..., so I will ...
In the future, I want to ensure that ...
It is evident that ..., and for that they deserve ...
It makes me realise that ...
Most of the time, I ...
My impression is confirmed by ...
Next time, I will ensure that I ...
Perhaps it would allow me to see ...
So, what is it that leads ... to ...?
So, why do some ...
Surely, it is not possible to ...
That way, my ... would/would not ...
The only thing I would like to have changed is ..., as this would have ...
This makes me think about how/why ...
When evaluating my ..., I looked at ...

connecting ideas within and between sentences

additionally; again, alternatively; although; as; as well as; at first; at the time/same time; because of; but; despite; especially; even though; finally; fortunately; furthermore; however; if ..., then ...; including; initially; makes me; means that; might be; of course; perhaps; previously; since; so; subsequently; surely; unfortunately; while

sequencing

meaning: putting things in the order in which they are arranged, actions are carried out, or events happen

things to know: A sequence can take several forms such as a timeline of events or a procedure. Events are arranged in chronological order usually from least to most recent. Each event can link to the next or can be one of several that link to a final event. A sequence or procedure shows the order in which something is done and provides the steps to the final product or event. The final product may be compromised if the steps are completed out of sequence. Things can be sequenced according to priority, importance, logic or coherence.

sequencing events

example – sequencing the events in Anne Frank's life and death

Annelies (Anne) Marie Frank **was born in** Frankfurt, Germany, **on** 12 June 1929. She was four years old when Hitler became Chancellor of Germany in the summer of 1933. He established the first anti-Jewish laws, an event which caused Anne's family, the Franks, to move to the Netherlands. The German Army invaded the Netherlands on 10 May 1940.

Anne received the diary that was to make her famous on her 13th birthday in 1942. **Shortly after this, on** 5 July 1942, Margot (Anne's older sister) was called to report for deportation to a forced-labour camp. **The** Franks, fearing for their safety, **moved into** the Secret Annexe where they were to hide from the Germans for the next two years. **During the** family's period of hiding, Anne made regular entries into her diary, with her last entry dated 1 August 1944, **three days before** the Franks were betrayed. **Following the** betrayal, **the** Franks **were** arrested and moved to Westerbork transit camp. **Within a month, the** Franks were transported to Auschwitz concentration camp in a sealed cattle car. **Soon after this,** Otto, Anne's father, became separated from his wife, Edith, and Anne and Margot.

In October 1944 Anne and her sister were transported to Bergen-Belsen concentration camp, where they both died **within** days of each other in March 1945. **After the war finished,** Otto Frank returned to Amsterdam and was given Anne's diary by Miep Gies, who had worked in the building below the Secret Annexe. The first copies of the diary were published in Amsterdam in the summer of 1947.

sentence starters

... and this was followed by ...
... less than a day/month/year.
... was born in ... on ...
... which concluded ...
A great deal happened before/during/after ...
After a significant amount of time, ... occurred.
After a significant period of time had/has elapsed, ...
After the ... finished/started, ...
At a much earlier/later time, ...
During the ..., (number) days/weeks/months before ...
During the first stage of ..., the following event/events happened/occurred ...
Events associated with ... further contributed to ...
Following ..., ... commenced.
Following the ..., the ... were ...
Initially, ... occurred.
It is hard to decide which came first, ... or ...
Meanwhile, there were several events happening behind the scenes.
Much later on in the story, it became apparent that ...
Several days/weeks/months/years later, ... took place.
Several key events that ...
Shortly/soon after this, in/on ...
The ... moved into ...
The first event that happened was ...
The key events in the order in which they happened are listed below:
This is/was closely followed by ...
Within a day/month/year, the ...

connecting ideas within and between sentences

after; also; and then (use sparingly); as; as a final point; as before; as long as; as soon as; as well as; at the outset; at the same time; because; before; each/every time; finally; first, second, third, etc; following/followed by; formerly; in addition to; in summary; in the beginning; initially; lastly; meanwhile; moreover; now that; on top of; once; previously; prior to; so; so far; subsequently; the next day/week/month/year; ultimately; until now; within; with the

sequencing a procedure

example – sequencing the steps in changing a tyre

It is useful to be able to change a tyre because flat tyres can happen when there is no one around to lend a hand. Changing a tyre **is perceived by many as something that is difficult to do; however, as long as you have** some muscle, changing a tyre **is easy. It involves the following steps:**

1. Apply the handbrake.
2. Switch on the hazard warning lights.
3. Remove the wheel trims.
4. Loosen the wheel nuts a little (this can be difficult, **so** make sure you push rather than pull on the tyre lever).
5. Place the tyre jack under the jacking point.
6. Jack the car until the wheel clears the ground.
7. Remove the nuts and slide off the wheel.
8. Put on the spare tyre.
9. Replace the wheel nuts and tighten as firmly as possible.
10. Lower the car and tighten the wheel nuts again.

* It is easier for readers to follow a procedure if it is written with numbers or bullet points. Sentence starters and connectives that indicate sequence are frequently omitted.

sentence starters

... and ... can be done at the same time as this will not affect the outcome.
... involved a defined sequence of events to which the ... closely adhered.
... is perceived by many as something that is difficult to do; however, as long as you have ..., ... is easy.
... to form the final ...
... were set up in the following way: ...
After ... was completed/prepared ...
Before beginning, it is/was necessary to ...
Before beginning the next step, ensure that you have ...
Ensure the next step is completed before ...
In the next stage of the (process) ...
Initially, check that you have ...
It involves the following steps: ...
It is important that these steps occur in the prescribed order.
It matters/does not matter if ... occurs first.
Make sure that ... is completed before ... commences.
On completion, ...
Once ... had been ..., ... were ...
Once ... was completed, then ...
Once the ... has/had been established/put in place/decided, then ...
The final part of the (process) is/was/included ...
The following steps are required to ...:
The next logical step is to ...
The second/next step involves/involved ...
When you have done ..., then you should ...

connecting ideas within and between sentences

after; also; and then (use sparingly); as; as a final point; as before; as long as; as soon as; as well as; at the outset; at the same time; because; before; each/every time; finally; first, second, third, etc; following/followed by; formerly; in addition to; in summary; in the beginning; initially; lastly; meanwhile; moreover; now that; on top of; once; previously; prior to; so; so far; subsequently; the next day/week/month/year; ultimately; until now; within; with the

solving problems

meaning: developing solutions to problems based on their causes and effects

things to know: A problem is a situation that is usually unwelcome or harmful and needs to be dealt with or overcome. Sometimes problems are small; other times it may seem that solutions are difficult to find. Problems have causes (what makes them occur); effects (what we can see that shows us the problem); and solutions (what can be done to make the problem go away). Before suggesting solutions, it is necessary to identify the causes and effects.

example – solving the problem of water shortages in Chile

The residents of villages, towns and cities in the northern part of Chile in South America **have benefited significantly from an innovative solution to the problem of** chronic and ongoing water shortages. They have had to live on 8 litres a day, which does not leave much for washing. This region is on the fringes of the Atacama Desert – the driest non-polar desert in the world. Only Antarctica is drier. **Despite** the lack of rain, moisture is present in this area from the Camanchaca, a mist that rolls in from the Pacific.

Even though many parts of Chile are close to the coast, atmospheric conditions do not allow much rain to form, **therefore** little rain falls. The onshore winds that come into contact with cold ocean currents bring enough moisture in the form of fog, **but** the particles are too small and fine to form water droplets.

There are problems associated with some of the solutions that have been tried so far to resolve water shortages. Water was trucked in from wetter places. **This solution did** provide water, **although the** supply was limited. Sometimes, the trucks would be delayed or did not arrive at all, leaving the people without water. The trucks were used for transporting other liquids, **so** the water was often contaminated. **Another solution is** desalination of sea water, **although** this is expensive because of the large amounts of energy required.

The most exciting solution to the problem of water shortages **has been the** use of fog catchers. These are nets made from polyolefin – a cheap, widely available plastic – that catch the fog. Moisture condenses on the nets, runs into storage tanks and is then pipelined directly to the villages. **This solution has been so successful and has** collected so much water **that** people now have running water, something previously unheard of. **Another advantage of this solution is that** water is obtained very cheaply **because** little energy is required. **The solution of** catching the fog or collecting water from thin air **is truly brilliant**.

sentence starters

... causing major problems.
... have benefited significantly from an innovative solution to the problem of ...
... is a partial solution to the (problem of) ...
... is an enduring problem in need of an urgent solution.
An innovative approach to solving these problems has been developed in/by ...
Another advantage of this solution is that ... because ...
Another benefit of solving this problem is the ...
Another/One cause of the problem is/was a ...
Another solution is ..., although ...
As a result of ..., ..., and this meant ...
As a result of these measures, there are ...
Despite the fact that the ..., recent times have seen an intensification of the problem of ...
However, not all results are positive.
However, we still need to ...
If the causes of this problem continue to be ignored, then the long-term effects will be devastating.
In recent times, the problem has become so severe that ...
It reduces the need for ..., and this is a further advantage.
One of the benefits is that ...
Solution A offers several benefits in the short term, but fewer in the longer term.
Solutions in the past to the problem of ... have not tackled the root causes; therefore, the problem persists.
Solutions to the problem of ... have eluded us for many years.
The ... problem is an enduring one, with ...
The causes of the problem are many and varied.
The most exciting solution to the problem of ... has been the ...
The problem has reached crisis proportions, and solutions, to date, have not tackled the root causes.
The problem of ... began to emerge about ...
The problem of ... has emerged over many/in recent years.
The solution of ... is truly brilliant.
There are many problems associated with Solution B, especially ...
There are plenty of examples from which we can learn about effective solutions to this problem.
There are problems associated with some of the solutions that have been tried so far to resolve ...
There are several causes of the problem of ...; therefore, a single solution will not suffice.
This means they have ...
This problem is one that is not easily solved because ...
This solution did ..., although the ...
This solution has been so successful and has ... that ...
To solve this critical problem ...
While the causes of the problem of ... are unclear, the effects are widespread and persistent.

connecting ideas within and between sentences

a solution is; although; and yet; another; as; as a result of; as there are; because; but; caused by; clearly; despite; even though; fosters/fostered; gave/gives rise to; grew out of; has reached; imminent; multiple causes; must; necessary; required; should; so; solution to; solved by; sometimes; spawned; tackle the problem; than; the effect of; therefore; to eliminate; to overcome; to reduce; to resolve; to succeed; urgent; when ..., then ...; whereas; which leads to; while

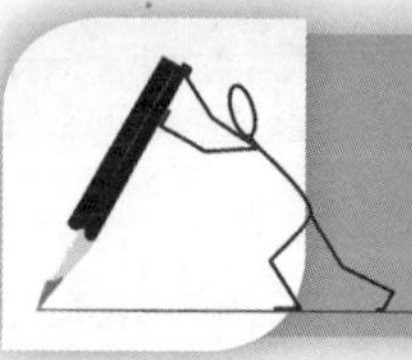

summarising

meaning: giving a short account of something with the main points but not the details

things to know: Summarising is selecting key ideas and leaving details behind. Main ideas are determined by purpose for reading. If the purpose is changed, then what was a main idea may become a detail. Before trying to summarise, it is a good idea to develop some focus questions or headings that will help with selecting main ideas. Note-making is an integral part of summarising, and it is a good idea to learn to make notes in bullet-point form. If the text is too difficult to understand, then summarising will be difficult. Remember that key words do not change when summarising; it is the way these words are put together that changes.

example – summarising the changes in dwelling sizes in Australia according to the 2016 Australian Census

Australians live in some of the largest homes in the world, with approximately 75% living in detached or separate homes, most commonly with three bedrooms. **However**, the 2016 Australian Census **revealed some significant changes in** dwelling size, **and they are summarised here.**

The general trend is for smaller detached houses to be declining in number, **especially** those with three bedrooms. **The main reason for this is that** much of the old housing stock in inner-city areas has been demolished to make way for other developments.

The new houses being built are still large, but the trend is for them to be smaller than in the past. Fewer mansions are being built. **An interesting finding is that, even though** households (number of people living in a dwelling) are getting smaller, house size **is not reflecting this. Generally**, people want more rooms, such as extra bedrooms, studies, media rooms and rumpus rooms.

One of the most noticeable trends is the increase in the number of medium- and high-density dwellings, which include townhouses, flats, apartments and terraces. **Most of these are** one- or two-bedroomed. **This trend reflects** urban planning measures to reduce urban sprawl and concentrate growth in urban areas. New apartments account for nearly half of all development in Australia, and these are located mainly in the capital cities. **One of the key findings of the** Census **is that** more Australians are choosing to live in apartments**, and this is apparent among** the 25–35 age group and 'downsizing' baby boomers (65+ age group).

Reference: Alexander, S. (2017, July 4). Is the way we are living changing? Trends show changes in dwelling density and house size. https://blog.id.com.au/2017/population/demographic-trends/is-the-way-we-are-living-changing-trends-show-changes-in-dwelling-density-and-house-size/

sentence starters

... are more likely in ...
... data shows that ...
... is a major problem that affects ...
... is generally regarded as ...
A conclusion can be drawn supported by extensive evidence that ... and constitutes ...
All ... experience some ...
All the evidence suggests that there is no ..., as a number of factors combine to ...
An interesting finding is ..., even though ... is not reflecting this.
Another key concern that emerges from studies is ...
Clearly, it can be concluded that ...
Crucially, ... is increased/reduced because ...
However, ... revealed some significant changes in ..., and they are summarised here.
However, one central idea emerges from studies, which is that ...
However, the majority of cases are likely to be found in ...
In many cases of ..., ...
In the majority of cases, ...
Many ... are ...
More seriously, ..., and ultimately, ...
More visible effects of ... include ...
Most of these are ...
On the whole, the factors that ... include the ..., more often than not with ...
One of the key findings of the ... is that ..., and this is noticeable/apparent among ...
One of the most noticeable trends is the ...
Significantly though, it is possible for ...
So, to restate the opening remarks, the key ideas are ...
Studies have shown that ...
The ... is well documented.
The central idea/essence of the argument presented in this text is ...
The evidence suggests that ..., including ...
The general trend is for ..., especially ...
The main ideas related to the topic of ... are ...
The main reason for this is that ...
The reasons for ... can be grouped into two categories: those that ... and those that ...
There are a few key/significant points that relate to the ...
There are a number of general factors to consider before ..., and these are summarised here.
There are two main ways in which ... plays out.
This trend reflects ...

connecting ideas within and between sentences

as a result; as well as; at a glance; because; crucially; essentially; finally; first of all; firstly; for example; for the most part; furthermore; generally; hence; however; in addition; in a nutshell; in essence; in most/many cases; in summary; include/s; main/mainly; most importantly; normally; often; on the whole; primarily; second/secondly; states; suggest/s; summing up; then; thus; to begin with; to conclude; together; to tie things up

synthesising

meaning: combining or putting together different parts or elements such as information, ideas or components to make a new or innovative whole

things to know: When new ideas, information or products are created, they do not come from nowhere. They are sourced from a number of places and put together in a new or innovative way. Synthesising is an important and complex skill. Unlike summarising, which is condensing and restating the main ideas, synthesising involves combining, comparing and contrasting ideas from several sources, to see them in a new way and draw your own conclusions. The reassembled material is original.

example – synthesising elements of design of a school backpack

School bags have come a long way in their design from the satchels of decades ago. Children have to carry much more to and from school than their parents and grandparents did; **therefore**, bags should be chosen with care. **The** 'Pack and Stack' carrier **designed by** Carryall Solutions Inc. **addresses some of the problems associated with** other school bags **and is, therefore, the** most superior design to date.

The best features of existing models include their ergonomic design; their many compartments to hold a variety of luggage of all shapes and sizes; and the fact that they can be used as both a backpack and a case with wheels. **However**, with handles that adjust to only one height, existing models do not generally cater for the growth of children throughout the school year. The 'Pack and Stack', **on the other hand**, has a handle with three adjustable positions.

Even though the fabric of the 'Pack and Stack' is fully waterproof (many existing models are only showerproof), the weight of the school bag is not compromised. **If money were not an issue,** the 'Pack and Stack' would contain compartments with hard walls, **so that** electronic devices would be afforded a measure of protection from the heavy use of these bags by school students. **One of the worst features of existing models is** too many compartments; **as a result,** the 'Pack and Stack' has reduced the number of these, **while** making sure that they are all fit for purpose. **This new design brings together the best features of existing** school bags, with some clever modifications that make it one of the best on the market.

sentence starters

... is an innovative use for a traditional object.
... point out ...
... we should examine ... practices so that we can develop ...
A second characteristic of ... is/was/has been ...
All evidence and supporting documentation points to ...
An examination of the facts makes this the desired outcome.
Another thing/feature ... have in common is ...
Clearly, it can be concluded that ...
Data from several sources supports the argument that ...
Finally, there has been a ...
However, others argue that, despite ...
I have used elements of style from several places to design ...
If money were not an issue, ..., so that ...
Improvements might include ...
It is surprising that this idea/solution/point of view has not been seriously considered before.
My recommendation, after examining all the evidence, is to ...
New and unusual ideas for ... include the following:
One of the worst features of existing models is ...; as a result, ..., while ...
One source suggests ... and another source supports ...
Research has enabled this conclusion to be reached.
Researchers are in general agreement about ...
Several sources have been used to create ...
So, to conclude, the elements of a successful plan to ... include ...
The ... designed by ... addresses some of the problems associated with ... and is, therefore, the ...
The best features of ... include ..., and the worst features of ... include ...; therefore, future models should include ... and omit ...
The best solution to the problem is ... because it takes into account information from several sources.
The elements of the design could be assembled in the following way:
The information from Source A is different from Source B because ...
The investigation showed ..., and as a result, ... is a better alternative.
The issue can be resolved by combining ... with ...
The new design addresses some of the problems associated with previous models and therefore is an improved version.
There are several ways to resolve the issue of ...
This new design brings together some of the best features of previous/existing ...
This perspective appears in multiple texts: ...
Various sources support ...

connecting ideas within and between sentences

although; and, as a result; because; but; cause/caused/causes; collectively; combines; consequently; drawn together; even though; exclude; furthermore; however; if ... then; in order for; in that respect; include; instead of; joins/joined; merge/d; nevertheless; on the other hand; so that; therefore; to blend the ideas; together; whereas; while

alternatives to 'said'

explanation

It is common practice in formal writing to relate what other people have said or written. To repeatedly use the word 'said' can be tedious and unsophisticated. The list below provides some alternatives.

acknowledged
admitted
agreed
alleged
announced
argued
asserted
came to the conclusion
claimed
clarified
commented
concluded
contradicted the commonly held beliefs
contended
declared
demonstrated
denied
described
emphasised
estimated
explained
found
indicated
made it clear
noted
offered a well-considered solution
offered an alternative explanation
opined
pleaded the case for
proposed
put forward the view
refuted
rejected
reported the findings
repudiated the arguments
resolved
revealed
showed
stated
stressed
suggested
supported the argument that
told
urged the reader to
vehemently denied

first person or third person?

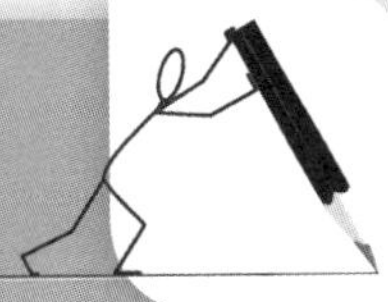

explanation

In most forms of formal writing, the use of the first person (*I*, *me*, *my* or, if the text is a collaborative effort, *we*, *us*, *our*) is generally discouraged. Excessive use of the first person can result in texts that focus more on the writer than the subject at hand. A text can have more rigour, authority or greater objectivity if it is written in the third person. In addition, the use of the passive voice (i.e. the 'doer' is removed) is a prominent feature of many technical texts. However, attempts to avoid the use of first person can lead to lengthy and confusing sentences.

In recent decades, there has been increasing acceptance of formal writing in the first person. The use of first person may suit the form of writing. In some cases, omitting personal references can result in fewer compelling statements, and may appear to be indecisive. In some forms of writing the author may be expected to describe their background or personal learning journey, or to give an opinion. Attempting to do this in third person sounds unnatural.

However, your school may have its own guidelines about the use of first person. It is sometimes a hot topic, and opinions vary. If in doubt, check with your teacher.

If you decide to write in third person, the phrases below provide some ways to avoid the use of the first person.

It could be suggested that ...
This is/can be illustrated by ...
It is seen through ...
This is evident when ...
Upon examination, it was apparent that ...
The facts indicate that ...
This is exemplified by ...
This illustrates that ...
This shows that ...
Therefore, it can be stated that ...

This becomes apparent when ...
With some exceptions, sources generally agree that ...
... clearly points out that ...
This is most obvious when ...
It can, therefore, be observed that ...
There is evidence to support both opinions on this topic.
‹Author 1› (‹date›) agrees/disagrees with ‹Author 2› (‹date›) about ...
The most notable exceptions to this rule are ...
Observations reveal that ...

degrees of intensity (modality)

MODE	LOW →							HIGH
probability	impossible/ impossibly	improbable/ improbably	unlikely	possible/ possibly	likely/in all likelihood	probable/ probably	sure/surely	certain/ certainly
frequency	never	seldom	occasional/ occasionally	sometimes	often	usual/usually	regularly/in most cases	always
certainty	never	scarce/scarcely	perhaps/in some cases	might/could	as likely as not	inevitable/ inevitably	undoubted/ undoubtedly	definite/ definitely
extent	never	scarce/scarcely	limited	partly	general/ generally	mainly	mostly	complete/ completely
confidence	suspect	unreasonable/ unreasonably	doubtful/ doubtfully	moderate/ moderately	reasonable/ reasonably	plausible/ plausibly	undeniable/ undeniably	irrefutable/ irrefutably
importance	desirable/ desirably	prefer/ preferably	require/required	necessary	important/ importantly	essential/ essentially	unquestionable/ unquestionably	vital/vitally
intensity	scarce/scarcely	slight/slightly	mild/mildly	intermittent/ intermittently	moderate/ moderately	typical/typically	unrelenting/ unrelentingly	extreme/ extremely

Caution: The adjectives and adverbs in this table are often used to convey an opinion. If they are used in academic writing, the choice of word would usually be supported by evidence.

task word glossary

accounting (for)	giving reasons for something and reporting on those reasons
analysing	the process of identifying and examining the parts of something in detail and discussing or interpreting the relationship of the parts to each other and to the whole; may involve description, comparison, explanation, interpretation and critical comment to determine the logic or reasonableness of the information
applying	using what is known and understood in an often new and unfamiliar situation
appraising	evaluating the worth or significance of something or someone and making a judgement
appreciating	recognising or making a judgement about the value or worth of something; grasping the implications of something such as a decision
arguing	presenting one or both sides of an issue, idea or case to reach a conclusion; may involve the use of persuasive techniques (logical rather than emotive) to convince others that your opinion, point of view or argument about something is valid; also includes reasons to support an argument
assessing	making a judgement about something based on its value or worth (may include quality, outcomes, results or size)
assuming	accepting that something is true without necessarily confirming it or checking its validity
authenticating	proving or showing that something is true, genuine or valid
calculating	ascertaining or determining something from facts, figures or information
categorising	dividing by sorting and separating things or people into particular groups or classes or saying to which set they belong based on common criteria
clarifying	making something clearer and easier to understand by removing any confusion
classifying	grouping things or people with shared qualities or characteristics into sets or deciding to which set or category they belong based on common criteria
commenting	expressing an opinion or judgement, either verbally or in written form, in response to a statement or based on the results of a calculation

task word glossary

communicating	conveying knowledge and understanding to others so that they are aware of situations and issues
comparing	examining two or more things or people and noting the ways in which they are similar AND different; examining the significance of the similarities and differences
comprehending	understanding the meaning of something and being able to convey that understanding
concluding	drawing together the main ideas of something and restating them in a succinct way, often as a decision; a conclusion may involve making recommendations for the future
conducting	managing and organising so that something can be carried out
considering	taking something into account before making a decision by reflecting and thinking deliberately and carefully about the topic or issue
constructing	creating or putting together an argument by arranging ideas or items; making or building an object
contrasting	examining two or more items or situations and focusing on the differences, referring to both/all of the items/situations throughout
critiquing	reviewing a piece of work (theory, practice, performance) analytically for the purpose of a critical appraisal which is supported with details
debating	examining both sides of an issue and coming to a conclusion or giving the reader/listener the opportunity to come to their own conclusion
deducing	reaching a conclusion about something based on reasoning, information and evidence that is known to be true and accurate
defending	arguing in support of something or someone
defining	showing, describing or stating clearly the qualities or attributes of something and what its limits are
demonstrating	proving an argument through reasoning and evidence; giving or showing practical examples
deriving	arriving at something by applying reasoning
describing	giving a detailed account (written or spoken) of the characteristics, features, properties, parts or qualities of something (event, pattern, process or situation) or someone
designing	producing a plan or model that represents a unique idea
determining	finding something out or drawing a conclusion about something after investigating, considering or calculating

developing elaborating or expanding on a topic by adding detail, complexity or intricacy

devising carefully thinking out and planning something by taking into account what is known or coming up with a new idea

differentiating identifying and showing the difference/s between two or more things and highlighting what makes something or someone distinct from someone or something else

discussing considering both or several sides of an issue or idea, without necessarily coming to a conclusion; supporting opinions or conclusions with evidence

distinguishing recognising and making clear the differences between two or more concepts or items

documenting supporting an assertion, claim or statement with credible evidence such as written references and citations that accompany the assertion, claim or statement

elaborating giving more information or detail about someone or something

evaluating giving a considered appraisal or judgement about the value or worth of something or someone by examining strengths, implications and limitations based on criteria and supporting this with evidence; making judgements about ideas, works, solutions or methods in relation to selected criteria

examining inspecting carefully and closely someone or something to decide their nature or condition; often looking for reasons how or why something may have happened

executing carrying out a task or procedure in accordance with a plan or design

exemplifying giving more detail about something by providing examples

expanding giving more relevant detail and depth about a topic or idea

explaining making an idea or situation plain or clear by giving reasons for both how and why something may have happened

exploring enquiring into something closely and broadly and discussing it in detail

expounding presenting a clear and convincing argument for a definite and detailed opinion about a topic, idea, issue or point of view

extending including or affecting other people or things

extrapolating taking known facts and existing trends about something and, by inference, using them as a basis for general statements about a situation or for predicting what is likely to happen in the future

task word glossary

finishing — bringing something to an end or conclusion

generalising — developing a broad statement that seems to be true in most situations or for most people; this does not include giving evidence or examples

generating — bringing into existence by creating and/or producing

identifying — noticing or discovering the existence or presence of someone or something; recognising and stating a distinguishing factor or feature

illustrating — giving examples of something to give more detail to information or more weight to an argument

implementing — putting something such as a plan or proposal into effect

indicating — pointing something out from available information

inferring — using what is provided to make meaning or arrive at an answer or conclusion; uncovering the answer, even if it is not directly stated, using evidence and reasoning

interpreting — drawing meaning from information presented in various ways, using knowledge and understanding; demonstrating a unique understanding of a text from the arts and using that to create a product or performance

investigating — examining or enquiring into something or someone to obtain facts and reach new conclusions

justifying — showing or proving that an answer, argument, response, statement, conclusion or idea about something is reasonable or necessary by giving sound, logical and plausible reasons or evidence for it; answers the question 'why?'

organising — creating order by arranging things in such a way that they are connected or coordinated; adding harmony and the potential for united action

outlining — giving all the main ideas about something and omitting the details

paraphrasing — restating what someone has said or written in a different way from the way it was first stated; the meaning is retained

persuading — attempting to convince someone to believe an idea or opinion or to accept a point of view and act upon it

predicting — suggesting what might happen or give an expected result based on the available information and what is known about a topic

preparing — gathering what is needed to make ready for something that is going to happen

presenting — putting forward something for consideration

proposing putting forward something such as a point of view, idea, plan, argument or suggestion to be considered for action

providing evidence referring to sources, illustrations and other evidence about something to support the points being made

proving supporting something with facts, figures and indisputable information

quoting repeating the exact words, usually by copying them out, that were written (or spoken) by another person

recalling remembering ideas, facts or experiences and bringing them back into thoughts

recognising identifying that something such as an item, characteristic or quality exists by being aware of it and acknowledging its existence

recommending suggesting a course of action for consideration by others and a procedure or set of instructions for enacting the action; providing reasons (usually the findings of an investigation or research) in favour of a suggestion

reflecting responding in a personal way, by thinking deeply and carefully, to something such as an issue, an image, a product or an action by making a personal connection with the information or ideas that appear

repeating saying or doing something several times for emphasis or to draw attention to the critical components of something

retelling repeating incidents or events that have gone before or happened

reviewing going back over past events, circumstances or facts, often with a view to what went wrong or could be improved

scrutinising examining or looking at someone or something carefully, closely and thoroughly

sequencing putting things in the order in which they are arranged, actions are carried out, or events happen

sketching giving the main ideas briefly about something or creating a sketch or drawing that shows the essential features; detail or accuracy is not required

solving problems developing solutions to problems based on their causes and effects

sorting systematically arranging items into groups by separating them according to type or common features

stating expressing something definitely and clearly

suggesting putting forward or proposing an idea or plan about something for someone to think about before making a decision

task word glossary

summarising	giving a short account of something with the main points but not the details
supporting	providing evidence and examples to lend weight to an argument or proposal
synthesising	combining or putting together different parts or elements such as information, ideas or components to make a new or innovative whole
tracing	showing how events or arguments progress and develop
understanding	constructing meaning from something to increase familiarity with the topic
verifying	backing up, confirming or proving a particular result with facts and evidence

my useful words and phrases

about the author

Patricia Hipwell MEd, BSc Econ (Hons), Grad Dip. Literacy Ed, PGCE is an independent literacy consultant for her own company, logonliteracy. She delivers literacy professional development to teachers in Australia, and works predominantly in Queensland schools. Patricia specialises in assisting all teachers to be literacy teachers, especially high school subject specialists who often struggle with how to combine content area and literacy teaching. Assessment has been an area of interest for many years and much of Patricia's work enables teachers to create assessment that is 'doable'.

The idea for this book came from the author's experiences with her own children who, like many students, struggled with putting what they wanted to say into words, especially when the 'saying' involved writing. It has been Patricia's experience that students need help to develop the language that mature writers use. In this book, there are sentence starters and connectives that students should use when demonstrating a particular writing skill. Language is the way that it is because of the job that it does, and letting students into the secret of this makes a significant difference to the quality of work they produce.

Patricia has developed a number of resources to assist students' literacy development. She is available to provide professional development to teachers to support the use of the resources, including this one, that she recommends.

For further information, contact:

Patricia Hipwell

Mobile 0429727313

email: pat.hipwell@gmail.com

Brisbane, Queensland 4075, Australia

2020

This book has been self-published by logonliteracy.